Also by Sandy Briggs

A God Experience In the Light

Merging with Socrates and Prebirth Memories

Shine The Light

Lessons from the Holy Spirit to Heal the Nations

Sandy Briggs

Shine The Light - Lessons from the Holy Spirit
to Heal the Nations
Copyright © 2017 by Sandy Briggs

Scripture quotations taken from the New English Bible,
copyright © Cambridge University Press and Oxford
University Press 1961, 1970. All rights reserved.

Scripture quotations taken from The Koran,
copyright © N. J. Dawood, 1956, 1959, 1966,
1968, 1974, 1990, 1993, 1997.
All rights reserved.

All rights reserved. This book or parts thereof may not
be reproduced in any form, stored in a retrieval system,
or tansmitted by any means - electronic, mechanical,
photocopy, recording, or otherwise - without prior written
permission of the author, except as provided by United
States of America copyright law.

Cover Photo by: Christina Swing

Interior photos and illus. by Sandy Briggs

ISBN-13: 978-0-9989579-0-6
ISBN-10: 0-9989579-0-9

Library of Congress Control Number: 12017906500

Printed in the United States of America

Dedication

This book is dedicated to all humanity, in hopes of bringing more clarity to a troubled world. May we all find peace, love, freedom and unity in the pursuit of our destiny.

Table of Contents

About the Author	viii
About the Book	ix
Foreword	xiii

Part 1 - *Initial Reaction*

Chapter One - Streams of Living Water	1
Chapter Two - Divine Visions	17
Chapter Three - My Call to Witness	29

Part 2 - *First Session of Epiphanies of Divine Revelations*

Chapter Four - The Beginning	41
Chapter Five - Dimensions of Creation	53
Chapter Six - Creation	61
Chapter Seven - The Living Mirror	71
Chapter Eight - The Mystery of Christ Revealed	79
Chapter Nine - Finding Unity with God	95
Chapter Ten - The Bridge	105
Chapter Eleven - A God of Wrath and Vengeance? My Thoughts	117
Chapter Twelve - Sin and Free Will	131
Chapter Thirteen - The Universal Religion	145
Chapter Fourteen - Divine Symbolism	163
Chapter Fifteen - Diversity and Traditions	173
Chapter Sixteen - Children of God	189
Chapter Seventeen - Let There Be Peace	199

Part 3 - *Second Session of Epiphanies of Divine Revelations*

Chapter Eighteen - Bridging Heaven and Earth	213
Chapter Nineteen - Clear Signs	239
Notes	263

About the Author

Sandy is a Board member and forum administrator for ACISTE (American Center for the Integration of Spiritually Transformative Experiences). She is also a member of IANDS (International Association for Near-Death Studies, Inc.) and volunteers for various organizations. Sandy is the author of two previous books and a wife, mother and grandmother.

About the Book

Shine The Light is a journey into the meaning and purpose of life. I learned where I had come from and where I will return at the end of my life on earth. I experienced a taste of Heaven and awakened to the remembrance of why I am here. I experienced the continuance of my life without my physical body and that life in the spirit world was more real than my life in the physical world.

I was not influenced by drugs, had no lack of oxygen to the brain and had no fear of dying. Before my experience, I expected death to be the end of my life, a closing of my consciousness into nothingness. Instead I awakened with a renewal of my life with purpose.

I was sent here with a mission to help our world awaken and to let go of their fears of death. Death is an illusion. Death is only a passing from this world to enter back into a spiritual world which we had forgotten. It's a world that is saturated with love, security, learning and compassion.

This book is the third in a series about the progressions that I had experienced about the unfolding of my awakening about life, God and the afterlife from a higher spiritual perspective. As I evolved in my understanding, I discovered more and more about the spirit and how Heaven and Earth are connected. I had discovered many answers about life which transcended religious dogma and the misunderstandings which had perpetually prevented most people from discovering their spiritual nature.

I discovered a world which revealed religion on earth as only a shadow of the reality of Heaven. I witnessed God and received personal revelations through visions as the Holy Spirit revealed secrets to me about Creation, how and why we came to Earth, and the purpose of life. Many of the things I share may challenge your perception of beliefs as I expose profound spiritual insights with illumination to help us evolve in our understanding about life, death and God. It explains why we experience pain and suffering in this world and its purpose.

The visions taught me things that I didn't know before and I seemed to be drawn into the visions as though I stepped through a spiritual door into another realm. I felt the presence of the Spirit upon me and it fed me information either through spirit words and/or spiritual images which are difficult to describe. My spirit was drawn into another time or place or another dimension which is beyond the earth's dimension. I experienced things that I could never experience in my physical body. It's as though a veil of forgetfulness was lifted and I remembered a past spiritual life from another world and I discovered whatever the Spirit wanted me to know.

The information that I received changed my perspective about life. When I discovered that I lived in Heaven before being born on Earth, I could really understand how resurrection and multiple life experiences are possible. I could have never understood how such a mystery could be possible until I personally discovered that our spirit is able to come and go from one realm to another. Our spirit is eternal and life does not end when our physical body expires.

I have learned so much through my spiritual experiences and divine visions that I felt were extremely important to share with the world. Besides, the Holy Spirit continues to nudge me with powerful visions which tugs at my heart with compassion to share! I found so many answers about some of the questions about life and the afterlife and the purpose of our existence from a higher spiritual perspective.

Shine The Light may assist you in your search for God. If more people could understand what I was given, this powerful information could help transform our world into a better way of living. If the hearts of humankind would be open to accept what I personally discovered, I could see a better future for humanity. I can't let all of this spiritual insight go to waste when it could be used to help us evolve into a more peaceful world. I know that each and every person is loved by God. Every person has something meaningful to contribute to the overall human experience. There is so much more to life than mortal existence.

Foreword

Experiencing God does not require that our writing skills be perfect. It's important for me to say what I say and how I share it because I do not want my testimony to be distorted or embellished in any way by any other person. I tell it as it is without any fluff. It is a journal written in my own language, including any and all structural errors in all my humaness.

This book has been edited only by my hand, but the testimony is true and is at the heart of its purpose. I testify to having real Divine encounters and sharing what I experienced and learned through them, to the best of my ability.

I see the need to share my testimony in an effort that may help humanity to evolve in spirit. You may wonder, just as I do, about why God would come to me? I am no one of importance, a fameless person, one who does not seek notoriety and shies away from public speaking, and yet, I'm not meant to be silent.

Even in this, there are lessons to be found and understood about God and life. There are examples in scripture where God overturns the existing order when God does as God wills and not as people expect. I feel that this is the case for my story as well.

God works in mysterious ways and there are always valuable reasons for why God does as God wills, beyond our comprehension and beyond our beliefs, until we learn why. And to those who have been and will be blessed by divine encounters, we are humbled and submit to the greatness of God's wisdom, power and glory. Not one person could ever compare to this ineffable Source which is all-knowing, ever present, and all-powerful. When God reveals to us, it must be in small increments because, even in small increments, God's visions are as a torrential flood from an endless, limitless vault of spiritual intensity.

My words fall short as I reminisce my encounters with this Divine Source which is so holy, pure and whole, that even while trying to identify who or what I'm describing, this often causes conflict within the hearts of people who identify this Divine Source by another title or name. Perhaps this is why God said, "I am that I am", or was it "I am who I am"? People struggle so, even with the simplest of words.

I have no intentions of offending anyone by using the terminology *God*, but this is the word that feels most comfortable for me to use, although my understanding of God may be completely different from what you believe or understand. But what should I use to identify this holy Being/Presence in a world of people who have diversified cultures and endless belief systems from countless branches of religion? God's message seeks to unite humanity, to guide all people as one humanity.

Among humans, we don't believe the same way, even among our own diversified branches of religion. People are grouped together, and yet even among ourselves, each clamors to have "the" one and only perfect religion. This struggle to belong to the only perfect religion has always been a stumbling block to humanity. It has been the instigator to endless wars and continues to be so.

Although I was shown many things about this struggle through divine visions, and I understand how and why our world became so intermeshed with conflict, I feel completely calm and blessed to know how God feels about our predicament. This is the reason why God came to me and revealed so much that I couldn't have learned through any people, from any one branch of religion. I had to experience it firsthand through the spirit to understand.

I see the diversity of religion all tangled up in knots by the confounding of misinterpretations and errant teachings through human-derived articles of faith. And yet, at the same time, I see the oneness of religion through the eyes of the Divine.

Religion is helpful to humanity when we see, understand and live through divine eyes. Yet too many people see, understand and live their religion through "human" ways, which greatly distorts the divine guidance. Human ways often lead us to do acts of violence, crimes against humanity, and to become involved with a growing destruction of life.

The delimma that I and so many other people who have encountered God face, is how to find the exact words that will clear up the fallacies that would end our strife about religious superiority. Will it ever be possible to adequately explain the Oneness of all religions which can bring us together? If people would and could see, understand and live religion through divine eyes, there would not be religious wars. That's one of the many struggles that humanity has endured from the beginning of human conflict with one another. It sprang from the struggle between human versus divine wisdom, between those who follow human leaders who teach religion with a human understanding without divine insight. They don't understand what this means, but they think that they do. They come from all walks of faith. They teach a radicalized, violent and prejudiced teaching which leads men to fight and to conquer through annihilating our human foes. Right there is evidence of the people who are not driven with Divine insight! God is loving, compassionate and merciful! May we be guided to the path of those whom God has favored, not of those who have incurred wrath, nor of those who have gone astray.

Oh, how I wish I could find the perfect words to clear this up in an instant! Although I completely trust the visions I was shown, I also know the complexity to explain to people who come from diverse backgrounds and beliefs. While some may understand my words, others may misunderstand through their own points of reference which differs from mine.

All that I can do is tell it as I was shown and explain what I learned through divine visions, then let it go to the conscience of humanity. I give to God the glory for inspiring and guiding me to write down in words the visions that I received. I do this not to gain notoriety, but simply because I have compassion and pity for humanity's on-going struggles and suffering.

Through my visions, I have witnessed a world full of enduring love, security and purpose, which is much different from the world where I live on Earth. The world that I call Heaven is my true Home and the world on Earth is my temporary home away from my true Home. Life on Earth is a journey where I had awakened through divine visions to remembrances of an existence before I was born. This sounds odd, and yet it is true.

This is how it is to those who have awakened into a spiritual state of existence. We are as one who has one foot on Earth and one foot in Heaven. We are caught between two worlds to assist in bringing Heaven to Earth. We have seen and experienced a world of bliss that people on Earth should consider and learn more about.

If you may be interested in learning more about what I had experienced and learned through Divine encounters, I pray that your heart and mind be free and open to take in my witness so that the insights may transform your life with better clarity and spiritual understanding to appreciate the wisdom of God's revealing nature. This book is for you, for all of humanity to become closer in sync to God through divine visions.

Part One

Initial Reaction

Chapter One
Streams of Living Water

Throughout my life I experienced different forms of spiritual encounters. They kept my heart open towards metaphysical mysteries. I now see how important they were as a foundation in my life so that I would be able to embrace what I was to experience later in life. I was on a roll of discovering extraordinary spiritual things through visions and divine revelations which intensified during a span of time during the years of 2000-2002. It seemed that the more I could handle, the more was poured into me. This time, the information overflowed.

I will begin my story on a day that remains indelible on the hearts and memory of many, many people. That day when I awoke to the news of an airplane that flew into one of the Twin Towers in New York City on 9/11/2001.

I watched in horror and disbelief as I learned about the news. I felt troubled and shocked as I immediately made a phone call to my husband who had just arrived at his work place. No one had yet heard the devastating news. I informed my husband that there had been a tragic accident and a tower in New York had caught on fire.

Just as he informed his co-workers, while still holding the phone, my eyes were glued to the television screen as I saw a live broadcast of a second plane heading straight toward the second tower, just as the first plane had done to the first tower. I felt alarmed that something had gone terribly wrong for the plane, I had presumed, to have gone off course and headed straight toward the building. How could this happen? What happened to the pilot? Did he go unconscious? Was there a mechanical malfunction with the plane?

I stared in horror as I watched with unbelief what looked like an incredible, deliberate act of terror. The plane showed no sign of averting this disaster as its wings tilted to glide not away, but into the tower. That was the moment that will remain a time that will live on in infamy. It was a deliberate act of violence against humanity. But why and by who? Who could possibly be so wicked as to deliberately target innocent people who had no warning about this attack of terror on society? I questioned and pondered how and why people could become so twisted in their motives with such menacing and destructive goals.

At this point in my life, I was having multiple spiritual visions about God, life and Heaven. I was consumed with the love and the lessons from the brilliance of God's visions. I was shown that God loves all people and that guidance was given to mankind through various people of diverse cultures. These people then formulated a branch of religion to keep the guidance as a continual manual to help steer humankind to learn about the nature of the Divine and to continually strive to live upright lives. Each were inspired and driven to keep the message alive.

I could see a thread throughout all of the religions that connected each branch of religion as precious pearls of wisdom. Each had truth which could help humankind to live in peace if all people would seek the oneness of the guidance from its Divine Source. But if people viewed it from their human perceptions, the guidance could be tainted by our human understanding.

This is again, the delimma and the struggle for humanity to understand the difference between how people perceive divine guidance through human understanding versus perceiving divine guidance through the eyes of God.

You may ask how can it be possible to perceive through the eyes of God, but it is possible and it has happened time and time again to many people throughout the ages. There is a clear difference in perception that only those who were shown through God's eyes, are opened to a heightened state of clarity that goes beyond a lifetime of studying and reading scripture. People may learn a lot from scripture, but it doesn't make as nearly as much sense as when God directly intervenes and opens our spiritual eyes to see. This is possible to all people, but we are not the judge of who God chooses to enlighten in this way. There are many reasons why this doesn't happen to all people on Earth. I hope to clarify this as you read further along.

With each explanation that I share, there is the dilemma of human assumption which prevents people from hearing what I share. Some assumptions originate from false human teachings in the past, some originate from misunderstandings and through brainwashing which blocks the words of their true message and intension. For me to explain as I was shown through divine visions, it may stir up and confront many of our established beliefs and cause friction and rejection. That is your choice alone, to choose to believe or not to believe, but I choose not to be silent.

As the days and weeks passed, I continued to ponder about the unbelievable act of violence that I witnessed through the television breaking news broadcast. I was dumbfounded by the distance some people will go with their distorted views of religion when I learned that the culprits were calling themselves Moslems (or Muslims) and that they were proving their faith through a type of Jihad for Allah.

Right then and there I couldn't understand how any person could come to such an understanding about their religion - especially when I witnessed the oneness of God's love through divine visions. Nothing that violent people do in the name of God, or Allah, made any sense to me. Those acts of destruction were completely opposite to the message of God's love, mercy and compassion for humanity. How could any human bend divine guidance so completely opposite to what God had intended, as was revealed to me?

One day in particular, after 9/11, I poured out my heart to God with all sincerity and from the pureness of my heart. I burst into tears and asked God if there were anything I may do to help people to learn not to misuse religion in His holy name to bring harm and destruction to humanity and to our world.

With pure intent, I had offered myself to God if I may be of use to help our world to find peace. Little did I know what would follow. My offer was accepted by God and I was shown deep spiritual insights far more than I had ever received in the past. These visions penetrated my soul as my eyes were opened wider and my heart broke with unbearable sadness. I realized how people do monstrous things in the name of their belief and attach their atrocious deeds to God as a divine decree when it was never so.

If these people would have known God as I had witnessed through divine encounters, none of them could even remotely blame God for such decrepit distortion of divine guidance. This is another example of the misuse of the message that was misunderstood with a distorted perception as seen and understood through human eyes.

About a week before I was given the mission to write my first book, I was shown a vision that was instructing me to take action to expose the misconceptions and errors from people's perception of religion so that they could see how their actions had been harmful and destructive to the survival of all human life. Once the misunderstandings are exposed, then people may have an opportunity to change their perceptions within their own branch of religion toward a heightened understanding which could lead people toward peace. When people can see with more divine clarity and understand that the misconceptions were but errors in human perceptions of divine guidance, then people can begin to live their lives on the path of peace and love which benefits all of humanity.

Thus, my intention is not to discredit or to remove any religion. I wish only to alert people about the harmful practices that they do which causes the opposite consequences of what God has intended for us.

It is clearly evident that the world that we live in is in need of peaceful direction. How can violent acts of hatred, prejudice and murder bring humanity any peace? If any one of us suffers at the hands of injustice and corruption, it is a plague on society and we all suffer.

A deliberate act of violence does not bring the outcome of something righteous. All of humanity suffers the consequence of violence and this brings judgment into play. Without human acts of violence, there are no calls for judgment needed to fulfill the law. It is when people cause deliberate harm to others that we bring consequences of sufferage.

The seed of peace begins within the hearts of men of good will. In my fervent prayer to God, I had good will in my heart. I sought God's help to bring humanity up and out of destruction and this is the message that I received.

All during the first week of January 2002, I received more divine revelations than I could hold. I felt as though Heaven opened up the flood gates and spiritual wisdom flooded my conscience, mind and heart. My mind and thoughts were overflowing with Divine words and information. I had received true epiphanies of revelation.

Before this particular event of down-pouring took place, I had received some revelations in the past. Each new found knowledge built upon the previous as building blocks. In the beginning of this particular week of January, I knew that there may be more revelations given at any moment in the near future because of the initial messages that I had received. I warned my husband that something extraordinary was about to be revealed to me and that it was very important. I forewarned him not to interfere with me when it would happen. I already knew that I needed to be left alone without any interference when this special revelation came. Never did I expect to receive such an abundant down-pouring of information in the spirit.

By the end of the week, when I awoke in the morning, I was completely filled with God's Word. I could tell that something very extraordinary was happening to me. All during the night while I slept my mind opened up and revealed insight and understanding from God's perspective. I saw visions about God's guidance, religion, creation, etc. It was a 'knowing' as though I was there and participating in the vision and yet I was a spectator at the same time. I could see and understand a deep mystery that could only have come from God. I had no choice but to accept this revelation that I held inside of my innermost being. It was so tremendous and deeply transforming that it would help the world if they would listen. The information that I was given was to plant a seed to help the process of restoring a universal harmony to the world.

When awakened in the morning, I literally saw words in my vision whether my eyes were open or closed. I had an inner spiritual eye that saw from another dimension. I felt awestruck as I played with my eyes for a while with this new experience. I watched the words quickly flow through my mind's "eye" in the middle of my temple. I don't know how to explain this unusual experience but I knew that it was miraculous. This experience reminded me of the Hindu people who paint a dot (Bindi) at the very spot where I was viewing these visions. This Bindi represents the "third eye" or the sixth chakra, which is the seat of "concealed wisdom."

What I saw was like a screen of words scrolling in my 'inner' eye.

I almost felt like a robot that was scanning words on a computer screen! The words did not have spaces, and they scrolled in a speed that was faster than I could read. I tried to pick out just a few letters. When I focused on a certain letter, I noticed that the scrolling slowed down just a little bit so that I could see all the positions of that one letter become bold upon the screen. The remaining letters faded. As I tried to pick out words, the whole scroll started to fade from my eyes. So then, I stopped trying to pick out words or letters and the letters darkened and the scrolling kept flowing. Still the scrolling was not at the speed that I could read because I couldn't identify the words without spaces. I was very surprised with what I was seeing. I didn't know what it was or why it happened. What was I supposed to do with this? I couldn't read it, and yet it kept scrolling and scrolling, but for how long? I just waited and let it do its thing. The scrolling continued for a long while and I didn't know what to expect next.

Then after the scrolling finished, I was shown another tremendous vision. I was shown a person that I recognized on earth but hadn't met. He was connected to my assigned mission that I recently discovered through recent pre-birth memories which I wrote about in my first two books. Somehow, I needed to get in contact with him, but how would I convince him of what was revealed to me? He doesn't know me and he lives so far away. I need to help him remember his higher mission. My mission is very personally connected to his mission. If I can reach him and explain what I discovered through divine revelation, this could help bring peace to this world. That is a worthy goal that I am willing to devote my life for. I can't stand a world filled with so much violence and fear. There has to be a way to stop all the madness! Although this mission seems hopeless to me, I have faith that with God all things are possible. I must follow wherever God leads me and do whatever I can to help this world. I was overwhelmed with the revelations about this man, truly another book's worth to explain the entanglement of details between him and I. I would have never guessed what I had learned through the spirit. More about this later in Part Three, Chapter 18.

As soon as this vision ended, I immediately sat up in bed, consumed with awe. How can I explain all that I saw and felt? It was early in the morning and I was bursting with information. I felt like a spouting vessel (except it was in the spiritual sense)! Maybe this is what the scripture is referring about the "streams of living water" which flows out from within. It was speaking of the Spirit, which believers in him would receive.[1] This emanation of information felt just like a stream of living water because it had a continuous flow with refreshing knowledge. I was given divine insight about God's guidance in my heart and mind, again just as the scripture said.[2] These spiritual events were confirming the scriptures. Not only were they enlightening, but they were fulfilling its prophesy. Only God could do that!

So much of what I received was similar to the information in the book of Genesis in the Old Testament. It also included information about the New Testament except it was so much more logical and obvious. It was so deep in divine truth that it overturned the misconceptions that people believe today and had followed in error for generations. I saw the deception and ignorance of despotic leaders who regulate and control religious dogma which prevents enlightenment. It opened my heart to see the hypocrisy, and the ignorance of bigotry and prejudice which remains to this day among many of the followers of religion. I saw how religion has been used upside down to ignite hatred and to instill intolerance instead of love and peace. The information that I received would transform our understanding about religion into a heightened way of thinking about scriptures while embracing a heightened perspective. It was so simple and logical, yet this world struggles to understand it. People fear change, yet change is the solution to what is needed to transform our world for the better.

No one told me what to do with this revelation or why I received it, but I couldn't keep it inside. I felt as though my mind wouldn't rest until it was released in some form of word. I just had to let it out! I knew that I could not fall back to sleep or do anything else until I released this information from my mind. I had to do it immediately because the words were gushing out of my mind and I didn't want to spill a drop of this most precious elixir. I knew that this information was meant to be shared with the world because it concerned the whole world. All I know is that I'm not meant to be silent. This information that I received was to help build a bridge that would unite all people in unity. This was a path to peace if people would listen and heed its warning.

It was 6:15 a.m. when I went to the living room and began to write. I grabbed my notebook and pen to write down what was spewing from my mind. It was difficult for me to contain so much divine revelation all at one time. I was like a little vessel trying to capture the down pouring of a continuous flow and my vessel wasn't big enough to hold it all. It was like trying to hold as much liquid in a cup from the downpour of a great water fall! There were so many different things pouring into my mind all at once. I knew that I had to give my complete attention to this divine pouring of information and I couldn't take my concentration away. My mind was so full that it was overflowing and spewing out with precious knowledge.

I felt love inside my heart when I reflected on the message. I enjoyed the love of God's Spirit interacting with me while I tried my best not to break my focus. Try as I may to keep my mind completely focused on the revelation, I could feel that my mind felt split in two when anyone talked to me. My husband clearly saw that something had happened to me. He kept questioning me and completely forgot the warning I had given him days earlier about this possibility. My attention was diverted by his questioning because he had a way of interrogating people to get them to talk. It was difficult to be aware of God's Spirit inside of me while it contrasted against the realm of earth at the same moment. I struggled to keep my composure calm, but I knew that any outside interference would ruin the connection of this holy union. I was caught in a dilemma. Very quickly, I reminded my husband not to ask questions, but to no avail. He asked only more questions with more persistance.

Any division of my attention had an effect on the continual flow of unfolding this divine emanation. The understanding unfolded within my mind during the process of quiet and complete attentive reflection. But if I spoke during this time, then I knew that I would lose part of what was continuously unfolding in my mind. If I didn't stop outside interference, then that would continue to divide my attention and I could lose even more information. There was so much information and when I was distracted the unfolding didn't pause. I tried not to talk and waved my husband away. But because he kept compulsively asking questions, I had to explain this to him several times as quickly as I could so that he would not continue to disturb me.

Unfortunately, he simply would not listen to my urgent requests. I felt desperate and wanted to cry out from frustration because I didn't want to miss any of the details that were flowing in my mind. I can't cry now! That would really distract this emanation. This was way too important and I didn't want to miss a drop! I had received more esoteric knowledge than I ever had before in my life and I knew how important the message was to have come from God. It was more precious to me than any treasure on earth.

I know that there was more that I could have held if I could have kept my focus completely connected to God in absolute peace without interruption, but that was simply impossible at home. I tried to figure where

I could go to be alone in peace and quiet, where no one would be near. I had to be alone! As difficult as it was, I had to take a chance to find a location away from home as soon as possible, where I would not be disturbed any more.

It was nearing 9:00 am and the Library was about to open. "Hold on!" I told the Holy Spirit, "Hold on!" I sensed that I had to hold my breath to pause the flow. I held it as long as I could as I quickly drove to the library, half in a trance, then headed to the farthest corner away from the front door. I headed straight toward a desk that had a dividing border around it. There were no other people nearby. I sat down at the desk, took a deep breath, calmed myself, and said a prayer; "Oh God, let me retain what you poured into me!" Then I began to write.

Two hours into my writing, my hand began to ache so much that I couldn't write anymore so I stopped to pray. "God, if you want me to write down the revelations that you gave me, you need to help me. I am willing to write but you need to take away the pain from my hand. How can I continue to write with this pain?" After I had finished my prayer, I briefly rubbed my hand and began to write again. The pain was completely gone! I continued to write four more additional hours without the pain returning. I wrote continually at the library from 9:00 a.m. until 3:00 p.m. (except for that one brief pause to rub my hand), until my mind finally felt just enough relief to stop writing. I had more to write, but I had released onto paper the major outline of what I had received.

Although I hadn't written down everything that was poured into my mind, I felt that enough was written that I could stop for now and pick up the rest from my notes. I was happy and in wonderment of what God had revealed to me. At that moment, I felt brave and sure that our world would see better days if people would seriously reflect on the words I had written. God was with us and actively searching for people who will receive the *Living Word*. Now I understand what was meant by that! I felt comforted and loved by the interaction I shared with this Holy Spirit. There was nothing I wouldn't do to help. I knew that I was trying my best and I felt that God was pleased. This book is a compilation of what I received during the first week of January, 2002.

There is so much to explain, and an abundant amount of questions to answer. I was given only a cupful, but I could continue to write about it for the rest of my life! As I searched through the scriptures to verify what I was given about the scriptures, my mind opened up and went beyond the delusion of dogma. I directed my questions to God and asked to receive understanding. My prayers were heard as I received insight from this divine Spirit which inspired me with divine understanding that was beyond anything I had learned before.

Now I know how God's messengers felt long, long ago. The fountain of wisdom is deep and continually evolves further and further into higher truth. I know that there is a plethora more to come! God was, is, and shall ever be, and divine revelation reflects the same. God has revealed to people in the past, continues to reveal, and will do so in the future. We can never know all of the answers and we cannot evolve in understanding God until we detach our minds from the prejudice of false ideologies in this world. We must keep our heart and mind directly focused on God to discover God's ways. He is the One who reveals (Jehovah Jireh), and we are only God's servants, working as one to bring news from above.[3] You may have ten thousand tutors in Christ, but you have only one Father.[4]

First of all, I'd like to say that if all of our questions were to be answered, the books in which would contain their answers would not be able to be held upon this earth.[5] If the whole ocean were ink and all trees were processed into paper, they still couldn't hold all of the information that comes from God. Therefore, my intention is to give deeper insight into what has already been given by God through divine intervention (through all of the prophets, angels, archangels and messengers). Divine truth hasn't changed. It just penetrates deeper into undiscovered territory waiting for anyone who has an open heart to discover it. One book or one religion cannot possibly contain all of God's guidance.[6] God's Word must come alive within us. Even the Bible predicted a time of universal restoration in Acts: *"Repent then and turn to God, so that your sins may be wiped out. Then the Lord may grant you <u>a time of recovery</u> and send you the Messiah he has already appointed, that is, Jesus. He must be received into heaven <u>until the time of universal restoration comes</u>, of which God spoke by his holy prophets."*[7]

Everything that I was shown was foretold in the scriptures. The information that I received was about a universal restoration. This may also indicate that Jesus will be returning to our earth soon. So then, we better be prepared and wake up from our state of denial.

I discovered that if we love God and don't stop searching for God, then the Spirit of Truth will come upon us and into our understanding. This was the most important teaching that all of God's prophets and messengers have taught and yet this has always been rejected by most people - perhaps because we didn't truly believe that this was possible. Along the way, this most important instruction has been superseded by the rejection of revelation, thereby preventing people from discovering God.

As I studied scripture from various major religions, I clearly saw that they all guided people to conform to God's goodness and to be <u>open</u> to divine revelations. It never indicated that we should be open only to past revelations while denying current or future revelations! So many people deny the possibility of receiving divine revelations today even when their misunderstanding is contrary to scripture. This has happened before with other messengers from God and they were met with violent protests and even murdered just because they dared to share the message they were given by God to help them! The people believed that when their prophet died, the revelations died with them, yet many prophets have died and others sprang forth time and time again! How could the death of one man prevent God from using another person? God does as God wills and no man can stop that. Rejecting divine revelation (*Baruch haba* in Hebrew terms, *Divine Barakah* in Arabic terms) is rejecting the Holy Spirit, the Ruach Hakodesh. This is detrimental for spiritual growth and understanding. The understanding and denial about this mysterious Presence has been a stumbling block which prevented people from finding God. Too many people reject divine revelations as if it's not possible today all the while they claim to believe in God. Then they wonder why they feel abandoned by God. God didn't die and there is no reason why God would stop trying to help humanity. God loves us forever. The only thing which prevented us from finding God is our own denial of the Holy Spirit. If we rebel against the Holy Spirit and tune out its message, then we are rebelling against God's help. So it's not that God had ever abandoned us, but that we had denied the Holy Spirit which the scriptures forewarned us about and to be open to receive.

    I repeat again because this is extremely important. Divine Revelation has never come to an end just because a previous prophet had died. Only the revelations which came through that particular prophet had ended because *he* died. The death of any man does not end or limit the power of God to do as He wills. That's just illogical and impractical thinking! If God can give revelations to people of His chosing in the past, what could possibly prevent God from giving revelations to anyone else thereafter? A prophet is not God. So again, the denial of ongoing revelation has been a stumbling block which has shut the door in men's faces of ever attaining spiritual enlightenment. How may anyone obtain enlightenment if no one is permitted to receive revelations from the Spirit which teaches us the things of the spirit? Obviously it was not God who has ended divine revelations, for I give testimony to the glory of God that this has happened even to me. Enlightenment is truly the way of divine discovery which is available to all people who are open to it.

"[I pray that God] may give you the <u>spiritual powers of wisdom and vision</u>, by which there comes <u>knowledge of him</u>. I pray that your <u>inward eyes may be illumined</u>, so that you may know what is the hope to which he calls you." [8]

Chapter Two

Divine Visions

In this chapter, I wish to explain more about what it was like for me to experience divine visions so that other people may be prepared if and when this may happen to you.

I sensed the presence of a holy, divine spirit come upon me and it communicated with a 'knowing' concept that I do not even know how to describe. I didn't audibly hear a voice explaining things to me in my visions, but my mind could see mystical images of *re-memory*, like telepathy, that at times I recognized them as *forgotten* or previously *hidden* knowledge that makes all things make sense. While I was only at the beginning stage of what these messages would soon reveal to me, I sensed that I was watched and that this Spirit searched my heart and mind for the opportunity to send more revelations when I was prepared and ready to receive more. I knew more was to come because I felt where the Spirit was leading me. There was a visual flow which had come from an infinite ocean of wisdom and it poured into my mind. To hold one of these drops was to be overflowing with insight. I felt that if I didn't get this mission accomplished, then God would search the hearts of humankind until this emanation could make contact with another person who would open up their heart to receive. The infinite divine ocean of wisdom will forever exist.

I first want to describe what I felt when I sensed this Spirit's Presence. Before I went to sleep for the night on October 22, 2000, I prayed and asked God to help me remember *anything* that I needed to write about. That very night I was awakened in the middle of the night and felt an urge to get out of bed to write, as I had many times before. As I sat in my living room chair, I was visited by this Holy Spiritual presence. Usually when this happens, I am given a revelation, but this time as I waited for any information, I concentrated on the feeling of the Spirit's presence. This time, I didn't receive a revelation, and so, I believe God wanted me to write about the sensation to give a description to others of what I felt.

When the Spirit comes upon me, I have a warm vibration or 'humming' sensation which radiates throughout my body and sometimes warms my feet. My mind feels attuned and drawn to the faint humming sound which I recognize as a *presence*. I cannot identify any gender. It is difficult to describe, but while I'm feeling it, then it is easier to describe. When the Spirit lifts from me, its sensation is almost immediately forgotten. As soon as I feel its presence again, I remember the sensation from when it came before. As I focus on it, I recognize the feeling as being 'drawn toward information.' If any information is given to me during this presence, I must immediately write it down, or the information will elude me. The information is never lost, but is drawn deep into my subconscious mind if I don't write it down while it is still in my immediate focus.

I was in this state of mind for about nine months while I wrote my first book. While I wrote, I also received remembrance from scripture that I've read before in the Bible. I felt inspired with support and evidence to what I wrote. I made a note of the scripture and then looked them up to find where they were located in the Bible. They verified my writing and sometimes lead me into further explanations and other dimensions of thought. It lead me to a point that sometimes radiated out into numerous ideas at the same time! This is very difficult to explain because my mind can only go into one linear path at a time while divine revelations are multifaceted. The information was compound with dimensions within dimensions, interfacing one topic with another. I received each chapter in this book at the same time, but then I had to divide it into separate chapters to explain each subject matter. Everyone of them connected to each other and I felt that some people may need to read straight through this book, and then go back to the beginning and re-read it in order to understand it better. Contemplation on your part is very important. You may need to read all of the chapters before you may be able to understand *each* chapter.

Sometimes I was shown visions and revelations just as my physical body awakened to its conscious state, although most nights around two a.m., I awoke to find my mind filled with *spirit* words. I got up out of bed to write for sometimes two hours, more or less. The spirit continued to feed me revelations as long as I pursued them. I felt energized and enthusiastic while I wrote. My physical body usually felt tired only when the words were spent; then sometimes I would crash and sleep a lot. Sometimes I could feel my physical body struggling with my spiritual body because my spiritual body doesn't tire. Sometimes my physical body felt my heavy eyelids burning for sleep and my body wanted to fall down from exaustion. Therefore, my spiritual body took a break from thinking for a while to allow my physical body to recuperate.

My husband does not understand why I say that I must get up in the middle of the night to write. He saw that I did not get the sleep that I needed and told me to just stay in bed. I could not stay in bed while my mind raced with a tremendous amount of spiritual insight. The words won't allow me to rest until they are processsed. I can understand why my husband does not understand this process, because this has never happened to him. He does not *know* what I had experienced nor what I had been shown by this divine, Holy Spirit and the joy that it gave me.

I willingly give up my sleep in exchange for the words. Each time

I awoke in the morning and thought about what was given to me, I was amazed and filled with awe. The excitement that I felt from this presence and the enlightenment from the spirit are what I longed for. It was a joy that I willingly gave my life to the service of God for the goal to help humanity.

Sometimes the visions that I saw did not make sense to me. They caught my attention because they were unusual and sometimes disturbing, but always deeply touched my heart. But, after a week or so went by, something would happen in my life that gave me understanding to the vision that I previously had no clue to its meaning. Something inside me just clicked and then I understood. Many of the visions were pre-warned revelations or premonitions which later came true, giving me evidence of its truth.

For example, about a week before I was given the mission to write my first book, I had a dream/vision that did not make sense. After I was given clarity of the message, I then knew that the vision was informing me that God wanted *me* to take the *action* to expose the misconceptions and errors from people's perception of religion. God wanted me to expose the trash that people do in the name of religion and to show it to others so that they could see its filth. Once the filth is exposed, then people could change their path to a heightened understanding. When people can see and understand that the misconceptions are errors in man's perception of divine truth, then people can begin to walk the right path toward peace. Thus, my focus is not in removing any religion, but alerting people about the misconceptions and harmful practices that followers of religions do because they just don't know any better.

I had another vision that troubled me for a long time. It was about a train. In the dream-vision which turned into a nightmare, I was following along with other people as they ran from inside one boxcar to another boxcar. Inside of each boxcar, the people changed costumes to disguise themselves. I thought that the people were playing a game; just a simple game of hide-and-seek. I followed them to join in the sport. Just as I changed my costume to match their costume, they would run into the next boxcar and change into a new costume theme. This continued all night long! The train was very long and they continued to change costumes over and over with each new boxcar. It finally got monotonous to me as the dream became a repetitive scene and nightmare as I tossed and turned in my sleep, yet could not awaken from the dream. (From the spirit, I had a knowing that all of these countless boxcars represented the countless variations of religion and their sects, each morphing into a new costume.)

At first I wondered if they were wanting to hide from me after I changed into their costume theme, but what would be their reason? Why did they keep leaving me behind? Finally, I looked behind myself and realized that they were not playing a game, but were disguising themselves to hide from someone who was catching up to them. This *someone* was coming up behind me! I kept trying to follow the crowd into each boxcar but yet I lagged behind to see from *whom* they were hiding. Then I discovered that they were actually trying to hide from God! All along, I hadn't realized that the people were not playing a game, and I was doing what they were doing! I then knew that I did not want to play this game any more. I was not disguising myself for the same purpose of hiding from God - that thought didn't even cross my mind! I did not *ever* want to leave God! I didn't know that they were *seriously* trying to avoid God by camouflaging themselves within each separated boxcar. But in this vision, God told me, "Go then. Go with them and find out what they are doing." I felt so sad at that moment because I thought that God may have felt that I, too, was trying to hide from God. I bowed my head in shame. But then, I knew that God loved me and *knew* me. God *knew* that my intention was just innocently playing and that I did not have the same intention as the others.

I felt assured that God *knew* that I loved God and there was no need for me to feel ashamed.

This vision was telling me that God wanted me to explore the different religions and to see for myself what they were doing so that I may help them transcend their thoughts to a higher perspective. All people need to expand their limited point of views of exclusivity towards a broader perspective of inclusive unity. God wants to use me to help all of them to *want* to return to a universal religion that included all people without borders. Isaiah 56:8 says, *"For my house shall be called a house of prayer for all nations. This is the very word of the Lord God, who brings home the outcasts of Israel: I will yet bring home all that remain to be brought in."* (Israel was not intended to be exclusive to just one group or culture of people.)

People do not recognize how their own belief practices are unfair and harmful to other people. They don't realize that they follow misconceptions that were handed down to them. Though people were given helpful guidance in their religion, they did not question their actions to see if they were in agreement with righteousness, justice, and truth of a universal spirit. We were told to build upon a good foundation. The foundation is the truth which is reflected throughout all things and places all things, (including all religions) in alignment under One Universal Source, regardless of what we call it.

I understand how the insights that I received through these visions and revelations remove the chaos and disunity of human fallacy. The difficulty in explaining it with human language is now the dilemma. It is time for the whole human race to rethink the foundation of their belief system within their chosen religion. We all need to face the fallacies which brought separation and hatred among humankind, and choose to line up on the track of unity, peace and love for each other with a universal perspective. Religion needs to undergo a universal restoration.

I understood through my visions that all religions were given divine truth, although no religion is practiced without some distortions. This is proven in the fact that each religion has many different factions within their religion and they disagree even when they read the same scripture. Only the interpretation which actually leads the whole world to live in peace and love towards each other without oppression or injustice is the correct path. God's will has always been to help guide us toward a universal unity of love and peace.

You may wonder how can all religions lead us to God when they are so diverse? Divine truth is very complex and too confounding to be contained inside of just one book or just one linear line of thought. There needed to be religious diversity to teach the multifaceted information of the Divine Mind. Also, religious diversity would help us experience the consequences of our misconceptions. The consequence of not living in peace towards a diversity of people reveals those who need to realign themselves for afterall, God created with diversity.

I understand how difficult and impossible it is to hold an ocean's worth of knowledge inside of one vessel. I can't stress enough how complex divine revelations are for all humans to understand. I don't think that any human can understand every drop that is poured into us. We can only comprehend a cup's worth at a time, and that cup's worth is still an extremely large amount of information to learn in one lifetime. Our explanations are only as good as we are capable of expressing it. People who learn secondhand from a messenger, prophet, or apostle are limited even further in their understanding because they didn't experience God's Word within themselves firsthand. Each person can only comprehend part of what a messenger relays to them, depending upon their own level of comprehension or degree of resistance.

Likewise, all people are not on the same level of spiritual maturity. A diversity of religion provided a variety of explanations which were needed to reach people from different perspectives, different cultures and needs. People tend to limit their perception of God and religion, then debar themselves from the information from other people's religion that they cannot comprehend. Thus, each branch of religion is a runaway boxcar that has been traveling on its own path. Isaiah 53:6 says, *"We had all strayed like sheep, each of us had gone his own way."* My mission is to pick up each segment of religion and get them to clasp hands with one another on the same track. Then, they can all find their way back together in harmony if we will focus on the things which we all have in common. The peace train is trying to come near. It has always been on the edge of darkness waiting to take us home. We just had to open our hearts to see it.

Even though I know that God had given me guidance through visions and revelations, I still find it difficult to feel confident in my abilities. I don't feel adequate to be given God's messages. I'm still in shock that God chose to send this information to me and to trust in me to share it with others. It's not *from* me, but it came *through* me. I'll just have to try my best to do what God is directing me to do because what I write has the Lord's authority.[9] I know that God is watching over me because I am reassured through dreams and visions to boost my confidence. I had the following dream/vision on March 17, 2002:

I saw in vivid, bright colors a large fish aquarium. It was about one foot wide by three or four feet in length, and three feet high. Inside, it contained perhaps ten assorted fish of various type, size, and colors. There were gold fish, two seahorses, one large round fish about a foot long, and a number of different types of tropical fish. (I felt that these assorted fish represented multifaceted levels of symbolism about different types of people, nations, religions, etc.) In my dream, I wasn't paying too much attention to the fish until I noticed a few fish dying. Then I was drawn to the cause of their death was due to a lack of food. (This meant that people's spiritual growth had become stagnant and needed nourishment.) I realized that if I didn't feed these fish, then they would all die. Even though they were not mine, I had to take it upon myself not to ignore their predicament but to feed them because they were unattended to and deserted. They were not receiving the spiritual nourishment that they needed. I understood this to mean that God wanted me to feed what I had been given in spirit to all people. I am supposed to share my visions and revelations with the world.

While I was thinking what I should do to help the fish, I noticed that the large round fish was attempting to swallow the little gold fish, and another fish was trying to bite the tail from another fish, and the seahorses were also in danger of being eaten. (This is symbolic about powerful people rising to conquer the smaller nations in war.)

There was a significant increase of activity and agitation inside the tank. I was in fear for their lives and reached for the fish food. There were different types of food varying in color, texture, and size. I didn't know which fish needed which type of food, so I grabbed a little of each type and sprinkled them into the tank.

This was symbolic of the revelations that I received to share within my books. I was given enough variety of information to feed multiple audiences. Different types of people need an assortment of inspiration and knowledge about various information. In a world of diverse views as complex as our beliefs had become, God needed to send a message which encompasses everyone since God wishes to help all people to come together in harmony in a united humanity. Some people will be able to digest larger amounts of information than others because some people are more knowledgeable and more open minded than others. The people who are small in their understanding about God would not be able to swallow the larger chunks, but those who can eat, will have it available. Enough information will be given through the revelations that I received for all people to learn something to benefit them and give them spiritual food for growth. I understood that it was alright if people pick and choose what they can embrace from my books and let go of what they don't understand.[10]

    As soon as I dropped the fish food inside the tank, the large round fish let go of the goldfish and diverted its appetite toward the food. As long as they were fed, they would leave each other alone in peace. Suddenly, the fish tank produced an enormous fish aquarium beneath my feet. The floor was turned into an aquarium swarming with countless varieties of fish. I could walk upon their glass tank as if I were crossing an ocean beneath my feet. As I looked down to view the fish, they were getting along peacefully and multiplied. (This means that the spiritual food that they needed was given to them and it helped them to prosper.) Thus, this dream/vision reassured me that my books need to go out into the world to feed the nations.

    Then, I saw a child place his hand through the front side of the previous small fish tank to pick up something that was lying on the bottom. This child's hand could penetrate the glass without breaking it and move his hand as though the glass were liquid. I was curious about this, but then noticed that the child wanted to hand me the object and lifted it to the top of the open tank. I thought that perhaps he was handing me one of the fish that had died, but as I observed closer, it was a plastic blue stick with an image of a fish at the top, like a swizzle stick used to stir drinks. Unfortunately I was awakened at this moment by my husband as he woke up to get ready for work. I was sad to have the dream/vision end, because I may have found further clarity about understanding what this symbolized.

    While I watch these dream/visions, I usually get insight and meaning out of the dream about its symbolism. There is a difference between this and using my own speculation. But since I was awakened before I received the insight about the swizzle stick and the spirit child, I am left to my own speculation. I really don't know why the child handed me the swizzle stick or the purpose of the swizzle stick. Perhaps this plastic image of a fish was symbolic to represent something . . . Or perhaps I was being asked by the spirit child to use the swizzle stick to stir the fish together to symbolize a blending of people, nations and religions into a unison of spirit. After all, scripture says, "*May they all be one.*"[11]

Chapter Three
My Call to Witness

Life is constantly changing and evolving while struggling against those who try to thwart change. Divine truth is constant and doesn't change and yet from our perspective it remains a mystery until our collective minds open to new ideas and advanced understanding as more is discovered. People do not know the purpose of God unless He reveals to us what He wants known. Knowledge comes with progression and God sends guidance when we are ready to evolve in the spirit. Spiritual phenomena occur all the time yet it is always under attack by people who do not truly believe in the spirit. Some people study about spiritual things, but they don't actually understand it until they experience it. If I want our world to find better days, then I must share the divine truth that I received with the world as I am called to do.[12] The light needs to penetrate through the darkness to light the way, for ignorance to evolve into knowledge.

Deception can be proven false when the right information comes forward to enlighten and expose misconceptions. I believe that there are many paths that eventually lead us to wisdom of the Universal Source. When each of us spiritually evolves on our own unique path, eventually we will find answers about our spiritual destiny, and if not in this lifetime, then beyond. Each of us must experience the consequences of our own choices whether to evolve spiritually or not, and no one has the right to prevent spiritual evolution.

I've found it very difficult to explain spiritual things to people who are not open to it. They stare like deer in the headlights. There is an invisible barrier that some people have from their fear of the unknown and their fear of eluding conformity. They feel threatened by anything different. Time and time again, God has sent messengers to overthrow the existing order. It wasn't to cause trouble, but because the existing order does not work!

Must men have a license from men to speak the truth when it reveals flaws in human ideology and dogma? We should be free to share what God reveals to us in freedom even when the truth rubs against certain beliefs. No one has the right to dictate to another person what they may or may not experience in the spirit. Men have no jurisdiction over God! If one hasn't experienced it for himself, then they simply don't know and they have no authority on the subject. God gives us authority by the fact that we receive it through the Holy Spirit.[13] When these mystical occurrences reach down into our lives, then there is a reason why they happen and why we are called to testify.

As I share my testimony, I do not wish to influence that my life example is the only way to find divine truth. I know that I am not the only person in the world who has had spiritual experiences. I have found others who testify to some of the same experiences that I have had. I sincerely believe that all people have the ability to commune with God if their hearts are open to discover it.

Many people long to know more about spiritual experiences and are open to explore it. At the same time it is a shame that those who do have spiritual experiences are subjected to ridicule and condemnation by closed-minded people. Their unbelieving minds cause them to attack what they don't understand. We don't want to be attacked for sharing the truth. It is difficult to stand up for the truth and to be brave enough to take the abuse for doing so. To boot, it is difficult to understand the phenomena for ourselves! My wish is only to share my experiences to bear witness to divine intervention. God is not dead. The prophets and messengers of the past have gone, but that doesn't stop God from continuing to reach out to help us. How could it?

I hope and pray that I may reach those who are open in their heart and have the curiosity to consider these experiences. This may bring them further understanding of things beyond our realm. When I was young, I wished that I had someone to explain these things to me. Who would have known that I would grow up to be the one explaining!

I don't believe that I could *ever* have imagined what was to take place in my life in regards to divine intervention because the knowledge I had received and the feelings that I experienced were different and beyond what we know in our world. I saw with spiritual eyes into another dimension that is not bound by time or space. I relived something that happened in the past, long before I was born, and yet lived it in the spirit for today's era. No matter when God intervenes like this for our world, it's always been difficult to share with closed minds.

An analogy: It's like a bird trying to explain to a rock what it's like to have the freedom to move and take flight at any moment. How could a rock embrace such an idea (if it had a mind to think)? The rock laughs; "How can anything fly?" The rock has no eyes to see the bird. The rock thinks that the bird is trying to trick him and so it holds onto his pride. He throws up a wall to block his ears and becomes reclusive.

This is why humans need a connection with the Holy Spirit to penetrate into our hearts in order to *transcend* us beyond where we are in our present state. We need to be transformed like a butterfly that escapes its coccoon. When we are guided by the Holy Spirit, we leave our coccoon behind that trapped us so that we can soar over our limited boundaries to discover new dimensions of life and new abilities.

I can relate to how other testimonies in the past and throughout antiquity were judged to be delusional and therefore rejected by men. Many people died as martyrs simply for sharing the truth that men in authority want to stifle and suppress to keep themselves in power. They never permit what they judge to be impossible, to be heard. They are the immovable boulders who block enlightenment. *"Their wits are beclouded, they are strangers to the life that is in God, because ignorance prevails among them and their minds have grown hard as stone."*[14] Who are they to throw stones at the innocent? Humans are inspired with curiosity to explore and learn. We yearn to know more so why stifle it when someone discovers something spiritual? How could humanity move forward without those who bravely soar amongst the hewn stones so that men could learn!

Thank goodness that the truth eventually seeps in and people learn. If we remain as dull as these rocks, we would have never discovered about aeronautics! Fortunately, some people were more receptive and inspired to inquire further in their search and this helped our world to learn and progress in many ways. We've gone beyond our human boundaries and have soared the universe.

There's no telling how much farther humankind will advance if we would be more open to spiritual truth. This is a confusing world and it is difficult to distinguish who or what is true. If we truly wish to explore the unseen realm, then we must keep our minds open to explore the unknown without prejudice. We need to be careful not to be manipulated by human bias and denial. Throughout the ages, each new found truth has been subjected to harsh criticism, suppression and rejection before it is accepted. Why must the bearers of truth suffer at the hands of ignorance? It only shows that ignorance fights against truth to stay in darkness and feels complacent in "not knowing". People choose to remain ignorant about the spirit when they reject it. That's why they don't spiritually grow, and yet it is their choice.

During the first week of January 2002 I was shown that the truth of God's guidance was built upon the foundation of diversity. Life consists of diverse facets of: science, math, language, art, music, etc. Needless to say, it was a foundation built upon diverse things and incorporating diversity in all things. Doesn't it make sense that to deny the diversity of creation is struggling against the foundation of life? Our whole entire world is diverse. Everything in it and beyond is diverse. Yet there is a harmony of universal unity.

I could 'see' in my mind information from the beginning of time that explains Creation in further detail than was told in the Old Testament. The Old Testament holds truth, while at the same time its spiritual knowledge was veiled to learned men. Now I see the value and the wisdom of diversity. Here inside myself, I have the key to some of the questions that all people from all religions and nations want to know and these revelations value all religions. But of course! It should do that because God created all things and has wisdom and power to do anything. It is a wonderful and awesome feeling to receive revelations from God about Creation! This illumination is simply breathtaking!

This calm and quiet 'knowing' was found deep inside my soul, and I realized that it always was there except my conscious mind would never take me deeper into my subconscious mind to find it. This revelation is so simple and yet so complicated at the same time. How does one explain the depth of God's revelations? It's as difficult to describe *what I saw* in my visions and revelations as it is to explain *what I learned* using clear, conceivable words. I feel as though I need to write an entire book to explain just one simple concept from above. Simple, because it makes all the sense in the world, and yet complicated because human minds are engulfed in ignorance and fight against spiritual evolution. If our world would see the truth that I have inside me, it would admonish the ignorance of religious bigotry. It would change our world into a universal world in peace if people would disrobe their self-centered bias, prejudiced judgment, and egotistical pride. They can perceive of God's goodness if they will come to understand that our world was created to honor our freedom and diversity.

People embrace the idea of freedom while at the same time infringe on the rights of others. They can't see their own hypocrisy. If we wish to have freedom then we must allow other people their freedom as long as they don't infringe on the rights of others. Once people cross the line to harm others then they have placed themself into the hands of the law of justice. As long as people are within the bounds of civility, each person has the right to pursue their life journey with freedom, liberty and justice for all. If we insist on confining people to our personal viewpoints through coercion, then we are taking away their freedom. That makes people rebel and our world never finds peace.

The world has always sought answers for peace. Here it is placed inside my being waiting to be revealed to others. I have the seed to sprout deeper understanding. I must share my divine visions with the world in order to help enlighten them from misconceptions. I must deliver the olive branch of peace to a world in conflict.

My first response at realizing what I had inside me was, "How can I possibly write a book from God's revelations about the understanding of the concepts of the Old and New Testaments as being absorbed into one? How can I explain the oneness of all religions so that people will abandon bigotry? There's so much misunderstanding and distortion throughout all religions that it's overwhelming to untangle the web. What would happen if I failed God? Would our world ever find peace?

I was shown God's plan for humankind and how deep this plan

goes to bring all people together as one. We can make this transition smooth but as long as people remain stubborn, self-centered, and close-minded this transition will continue to be an arduous journey. If people would learn to be tolerant and embrace the depth of diversity within all things, they will see the light that radiates truth throughout all things.

I wish for all people to truly discover God in the spirit and to see what I saw. My spiritual experiences were absolutely amazing because they taught me things that I couldn't have learned any other way. I realize that there are billions of different point of views because no two people think exactly alike. Therefore, I can only share what I had experienced and then leave it to the conscience of others to choose of their own free will whether to accept my testimony. God's ways are too immense to fathom all at once and each individual is at different levels of understanding and each uses their own internal gauge to decipher which things they accept. The truth cannot be forced, for that only builds a wall that repels against it. Truth and freedom are united on the same side as righteousness. Anyone who doesn't believe the testimony of a sincere witness doesn't fully embrace their truth because it is in conflict with their own preconceived ideas. That's fine and that person doesn't have to embrace it, but let the truth be told and set free to land on those who can and will embrace it.

It is a long journey ahead for me to process what God has given me into an interpretation of language. As I attempt to share my story, I know that however I try to describe what I went through would never explain it adequately or do it justice. Our vocabulary does not contain such descriptions of the spirit realm because it is not experienced in the physical realm of existence. How can one define what others do not understand about the spirit realm when there is no connection to this comprehension? Words are used to express our thoughts but communication is understood only when our words are felt and understood by others through a common association. Now I understand more clearly why there remains such a gap about the mysteries of God and the difficulty for messengers to explain spiritual guidance.

My spiritual experiences help me to understand how other messengers and apostles of the past have felt because I have stepped into their shoes. I have become one in faith and purpose to bring the light of unity to humankind. This has also helped me to understand the scriptures of many branches of religion with more depth. It's incomprehensible for me to be considered to be one among many of the other messengers. Yet I realize that those people were but ordinary people like myself, chosen by God to reveal His guidance. I was called only to explain to the world what I was shown and then let others use their own sense of reason and will to follow what they will.

While this information helps explain our world with deeper understanding, I can see that it is still the same concept that was already given to other messengers and prophets. It really isn't anything different from what God guided in the past! It's just that humankind has difficulty comprehending it and therefore, came away with diverging opinions. These diverging opinions have become the obstacle of peace because their hearts were lead by an improper perspective. I can understand this so clearly, and I know that only a week before this experience I had not known. I have an ocean-worth of revelation to explain and yet if a person understood it, then this concept would be so simple. People should see that God tried to help us all along. The truth of God's wisdom shines while it is veiled to our mind. We must find a way to penetrate through that veil in order to find understanding. Jesus was the forerunner through the veil, and we are supposed to follow through the veil as well.[15]

It is with my sincere wishes and pleading from my heart that I beg all people to search deep within themselves and to reflect deep within all of manifested creation to see the Truth of God's Word in all things. I have a huge task to accomplish for God and if I focus on this task as being what it truly is, then I get overwhelmed and perplexed.

    We are all in this world together. We can learn to live together in peace if we will heed God's warning or we can continue to struggle against it and continue to live in a world divided by conflict. No one needs to abandon their religion, but we need to understand it with a higher vision which unites all religions and all people as one. When people's hearts are united in the same purpose of good will, we can live together in peace. If we sincerely wish our world to reflect peace, then our hearts must accept a diversity of all people who are civil toward one another. Each person contributes to the positive or negative energy of this world. The more positive energy that is released, the more peaceful our world will become. We have the ability to find peace only if we seek peace in unity of the heart.

Part 2

First Session of Epiphanies of Divine Revelations

Chapter Four

The Beginning

Let's begin sharing what I received from the Holy Spirit. The following was revealed to me about God's thoughts of Creation before anything as we know existed. I let the vision play out in its entirety as a detached observer who was drawn into a 'time before time'. I saw the unfolding of the birth of humankind's beginning to the possible goal of God's desire. I say *possible* because of the freedom God gave to human free will. I have the understanding within my heart, but the task of deciphering it onto paper and into a language is a challenge for me to clearly explain what I had received. Through my use of language, I express through gender by using "he/she" which is difficult to use while explaining this vision. The Creator had an equal balance of the masculine and feminie mind. Sometimes I was drawn toward the masculine side, sometimes toward the feminine side, and sometimes neither gender. I also use "God" to identify this Beginning Source of Consciousness from which all of Creation derives.

To the best of my ability to express in words, this was how the vision unfolded...

I was among two thoughts having a discussion, like among two hemispheres of the brain except there was no form. It was dark and yet it was not dark. It was both at the same time, like a static image of lightness and darkness. I couldn't see anything and yet I did perceive from inside a conscious mind. I felt what these two thoughts discussed and I became drawn into it like an observer and a participant at the same time. I sensed no boundaries and yet I didn't move. I didn't want to move. I observed two perspectives that were merged in harmony as one. I felt the masculine perspective on the top left and the feminine perspective on the top right, and I felt connected to both when each had something to think to share with the other perspective thought. It was like the left and right side of a brain communicating with each other and I was among them as a witness while this Consciousness was One – even with my presence. This is very difficult to describe! I was like one pinpoint of consciousness among infinite pixels of a formless static screen. Each pixel was a point of consciousness, although I did not sense any involvement with the other pixels. My focus was drawn to the discussion. I just watched in awe and amazement as I was drawn into this conversation.

The left side of this Consciousness was completely content and calm, completely tranquil and peaceful. The right side was also just as amiable and yet the feminine side wanted to love something. The feminine essence wanted expression of her love and movement, and an interaction with life to nurture and to interact with it. There was nothing to hold, nothing to see, and nothing happening except thought. Although the masculine side was quite satisfied with the way it was, he also wanted to please the feminine side and so began the discussion of her thought. The conscious mind discussed what they wanted to bring into beingness. Both perspectives wanted something to be like itself. *"Then God said; 'Let us make man in our image and likeness."* [16]

God knew that anything was possible to create, but first, it needed to be decided what *they* wanted Creation to be before it became manifest. I wasn't shown whether there had been a previous mortal creation but I sensed that God was already knowledgable about creating things which were limited and simple to create without being eternal. It was just a "given" that God knew this well and didn't need to expound on further while I was observing this discussion at this time. I did catch on that if God chose not to reflect the essence of eternal life into Creation, then it would be mortal because that Creation would not be able to simulate God's attribute of eternity. God has the power to share however much Divine attributes as God wishes and Creation would reflect back in life what God chose to pour into it.

Since God is eternal and boundless without limit and with complete freedom, I felt God's desire to want this Creation to reflect eternal life and free will. It was so precious to God to be able to share all that God is and to be *known* by Creation. (Somehow the word "known" doesn't accurately describe what I'm wanting to say but I don't know a better word.) Love is the beginning emotion that wanted to be shared as well as to be reciprocated. What reflected out would also be reflected back, like a mirrored image of invisible traits, except manifested into a form to make it unique.

Although there wasn't anything else, the interplay of this thought process knew that it needed to produce something other than itself, otherwise there would not be another existing thing. It's like air beside air; when there is no separation it is just itself.

The discussion encompased every aspect from beginning to an end goal before it ever made any movement. The goal was to have something *other* than God to have life that interacts with God. In order to bring something from Divinity into existence, there had to be a parting and a duplication of Divine attributes and a way to keep that part set aside or contained within some type of vessel. It's like blowing air into a balloon. There is air on the inside and air on the outside, yet they are separated by the 'skin' of the latex balloon. God wants a likeness of divinity within the form and yet it would need to be somehow different from what already is

God, so that it would come into being and manifest as an individual entity with the freedom to think as it wished.

The discussion then thought about its own characteristics, abilities, and essence that is what God is. God reflected on him/herself (no gender detected) and identified the infinite attributes of what is God. God identified the attributes of eternal existence (life), intellect (thought with wisdom and understanding), love and compassion (emotions), will (power), infinity, boundlessness (choice and freedom), endurance, goodness, contentment, etc. As God reflected on these attributes, perfection and bliss was recognized. Everything that God is, is good. The Creator was willing to share all of it's attributes with Creation. It was also understood that in order to bring something of God's likeness into existence, then the other likeness needed to reflect these same divine essences and yet be different in some way.

While I observed, I had an awareness that the Creator could ensemble diverse combinations of Divine essences into different living forms. A myriad of living forms could be designed with each creature being a diverse expression of God in unique combinations of God's own attributes. This is satisfactory and pleasing, yet all of these life forms would not resemble God in fullness. God wanted a closer likeness.

For a living being to have God's fullness of attributes and yet be different from what is already absolute perfection, is to accept and tolerate some kind of imperfection. This Creation could not be completely perfect or it would not be identified as an individual being. God pondered on this and saw that the Creation would not be completely perfect and yet wanted Creation to be as near as possible to perfection as it could possibly be without needing to totally merge back. This Divine Consciousness pondered how it could help Creation to compensate for its imperfection which also satisfied the desire for involvement with Creation. In order to create something that wasn't absolutely perfect in Divine perfection, there needed to be a concealment of something that was hidden or held back from Creation which made it incomplete and yet almost whole.

Both perspectives then reflected in thought about this concealment. To conceal is to hide (keep back) something from its perfection in order to create something different from God. The masculine side needed to reflect himself onto the feminine side while concealing something that he is in order to bring it into being. But to conceal something of himself is to hide the totality of God's entire perfection from Creation. This was a dilemma because God wanted to be known by Creation. But for Creation to completely know God was to know perfection and then Creation would not be separated from God as an independent entity, and therefore not manifested as God had wanted this Creation to be. So God thought further on how to reflect into Creation without being completely disclosed. God speculated very carefully about which aspect of perfection should be concealed from all Creation.

To give Creation eternal life, God would need to conceal *themself* while emanating invisible attributes throughout Creation to bring forth a manifestation that was different. God foresaw the essence of concealment and how it would bring into life a veiled enigma. So then God chose to build Creation upon the foundation of logic and truth so that there would be evidence to prove what God is without being seen.

While God would be hidden from Creation, both hemispheres could interact with it by revealing themself through Creation. And since Creation would not completely know God in totality, then we would not be all-knowing. Complete knowledge of all things would be concealed from us yet remain eternally in God. God didn't want us to be ignorant, but needed to create something of *their* likeness through concealment. Unfortunately, not to be all-knowing is to have some ignorance and so complete knowledge (omniscience) would be veiled. Only God is omniscient.

God then knew that there was a way to combat the lack of knowledge by helping us discover the unknown. God planned on revealing things to his Creation by increments, in various ways, thus Creation could evolve and expand as they were able. While God is infinite and boundless, physical Creation would be bound or limited in a form so that it could exist as a separate entity from its Source. To be bound is to have restrictions and so we could not contain infinite knowledge within ourselves while we were confined in a limited material form.

God wants Creation to be free and to also reflect the attributes of eternal existence and free will. So God reflected on how to combat our restrictions by permitting Creation to learn and expand in knowledge at its own pace and with freedom of choice to learn what we could grasp. This would also reflect a continual evolution to learn, grow, and expand in wisdom. And while our knowledge expanded, we would become more knowledgeable about God because God's invisible attributes would be revealed throughout Creation. Therefore, this is how God could be known while being unseen.

So, to begin the process of creating something different from what is already pure in perfection, is to become a different existence, thus Creation is always different from God while being of God. God is God just as fire is fire, or air is air, or water is water. God does not become less of its essence by giving its qualities to Creation. It's like separating fire from fire; or air from air, or water from water. The essence of fire is still fire when it is separated, but to keep fire separate from the original source, it needs some way to attach itself to another object (like a stick, match, or wick) or placed into a containment of form.

Fire is dependent on air to keep it aflame. Water consists of

The Beginning

hydrogen and oxygen (air). So air was the first element which came from God. Air provided an element for space or expansion from the will to move. Water came forth as a malleable element for movement (action). Then fire (spirit) came to emanate light (knowledge) to shine onto the water. These three elements are the beginning foundation of life, yet they had a beginning source.

For God to begin to duplicate divine characteristics, both hemispheres needed to share part of theirself and then place that duplicate part into a form or a vessel. So God would need to start the process by moving its stillness into action of will.

The masculine and feminine mind agreed to bring Creation into existence even with the awareness of imperfection and ignorance. They saw imperfection and ignorance as a way to become involved with Creation by nurturing it to evolve toward perfection and knowledge. So imperfection and ignorance is to be tolerated while we evolve. God also saw that ignorance will eventually bring about sin because sin is the action of doing harmful things due to ignorance. Sin was not perfection and it sows corruption. This was a process that God did not like yet also saw that knowledge dissolves ignorance and so there is a remedy. Ignorance is not knowing, therefore to know is to overcome ignorance and God would disclose knowledge to us as we were able to embrace it. It would be our responsibility to use our free will to seek knowledge in whichever area we were motivated to learn.

When Creation evolves with knowledge and understands the consequences of sin, then we could combat corruption through discipline and restraint. God would also bring into existence spiritual beings, which were not bound to the material world, to assist us to overcome our mistakes. God foresaw that the things of the spirit would defeat the lower nature of sin. The spirit was of life while the nature of sin lead to a temporary state of mortality. Life would conquer death. Manifested life would be the intertwining of the two, spirit and flesh. Although humans have the free will to choose between the things of perfection and goodness, or the things of corruption and wrongdoing, God would help guide us to the path of perfection. So God thought through this before acting upon creating which would permit sin to come temporarily until we overcame it. God saw Creation as a way to express him/herself and to share all that he/she is in love.

Since God's attributes are so diverse, a variation of expressions of divinity were placed into a variety of forms. Thus these forms held different combinations of God's attributes in various amounts of simplicity and complexity. The simple manifested life forms begin with simple abilities and are less complex, such as the amoeba. The more complex manifested forms then expand on upward into the complexity found in humans. The more complicated life forms have the ability to do multiple tasks. Humans are more advanced life forms on Earth because of their mental reasoning and processing capabilities, multiple physical and spiritual abilities, and the will to expand in wisdom and multiple other areas.

Humans were created as intelligent and emotional beings which reflect a great quantity of God's attributes manifested into the earth's physical life form. We are the expression of most variations of Creation combined into a being on Earth. We reflect the spiritual and the physical, the seen and the unseen. We contain elements which reflect the attributes that are found in planets and celestial things, plants which grow and produce seeds, and animals which animate life with mobility and voice. We were created from the life force and of the substance that does not have the movement of life which is like the clay of the earth substance. If the life force is taken away from the body, a corpse remains. A corpse is made of a substance that does not have movement. The flesh is like the dirt which is a substance that is not a living, moving thing without the life force. A body comes to life when it contains the life force (spirit) within.

The whole of Creation infinitely expresses various ways of existence through different combinations as manifested as the solar system, plants, rocks, animals, etc. Then within each of these, there are other dimensions of variety which shows different colors, sizes, shapes, etc. There are levels within dimensions which expresses individuality through diversity. God was pleased.

Then I intuitively discerned the right side of God's hemisphere softly move herself so that the process of creating could begin. She needed to bend and fold herself in order to reflect onto the left hemisphere like a malleable mirror. The masculine hemisphere stayed as he was while the feminine hemisphere moved herself downward, toward the masculine hemisphere, like a gentle wave and twisted outward until they almost separated. Then while they were still connected, they reflected on each other like the yin/yang symbol. This process began a polarization of God's attributes by reflecting his invisible attributes onto and into his reflection that was turned in the opposite direction, producing a complimentary balance. There became a stillness and movement, a sense of direction of up and down, and an inward and outward expression. Then everything that God contemplated came to be in the order of its disclosure and it radiated throughout all things.

The formless, static perception that I had at the beginning of this vision separated into two opposite but complimentary qualities of lightness and darkness. Next, the upper and lower reflection of the masculine and feminine essences produced infinite dimensions to reflect levels within levels. The light reflected and shined like water glistens, and so the upper water reflected onto the lower water which created upper and lower realms in the light and into the darkness.

Image by Sandy Briggs

Another dimension of reflection is how the eye reflects an image inside the eye but the image is turned upside down and projects to the retina before the brain turns it right side up again. Also, creatures have two eyes that reflect or think with the one mind. This is simulating the left and right sides of the Divine Consciousness and why our brain has a left and right hemisphere.

Humans also perceive understanding with the eye of reason. Knowledge comes down from above (from the divine consciousness) to enlighten what we didn't previously perceive. Humans uniquely reflect this invisible attribute when we use our brain to think with reason and logic. This is a natural process that guides humankind to seek a higher destiny. When we find a spiritual connection to the higher consciousness, God blesses us with visions and information which emanates downward into our mind with things beyond our present knowledge and capabilities. Intelligence prevails over ignorance and this is the whole purpose why God wants us to reconnect and learn. We are intelligent beings and we are supposed to question things and always seek deeper wisdom.

Humans are like gems to God when we radiate beauty and goodness at our highest splendor. The most upright of humans reflect the highest human potential which is the nearest to perfection as a human may evolve. Thus all things may freely evolve upward in spirit as we conquer the lower gradients of ignorance. We may become what we want to become from our own will while we evolve in the spirit. We could continually reach for perfection which is a good thing, and so Creation came to be.

Chapter Five

Dimensions of Creation

As I was absorbing the information from the divine down-pouring of the Holy Spirit, the visual insight wove back and forth, linking one thought to another thought. I was watching a point expand by adding and multiplying (like cell division) into a diversity of shapes, sizes and dimensions and morph into numbers and mathematics, science, etc. At the same time, I watched colors morph from the primary colors to secondary colors, then multiply into infinite colors, morphing again and again into diverse areas. It was very quick and yet it was the unfolding of manifested life itself in a blink of an eye. Everything was related and overlayed on top of each other. Everything had an order with relationships that were either drawn toward or away in variations of characteristics.

I witnessed the astral dimension of the sun, moon, stars, planets, etc. Everything reflected a spiritual reflection of the essence of God within Creation. The sun is a reflection of the properties of the Holy Spirit that shines light onto Creation just as the sun's light shines onto the moon, stars, and planets. It's a reflection of the creation process that I'll explain in further detail in chapter six. Then, the light shined upon the upper and lower realms. This branches into the dimension of the angels and all that is in heaven, and the dimension of humankind and all that is on the earth.

Within each dimension is another dimension that is contained inside the other, like building layers upon layers of infinite things. Our planet is one dimension and there are other dimensions which are the various expressions of life which grows on and in the earth. Plants are nourished by the soil, but not without the continual properties of the sun, water, and air to assist the continuance of the plant's life. A life form has an outer shell, and the inner area of cells, protoplasm, molecules, DNA, the essence of life, etc. The outer shell is the physical body which places a boundary around the inner life force of expression. The inner essence is the actual sentient life which thinks, feels emotions, and gives birth to self expression. These physical bodies consist of organs which: see, hear, feel, smell, and taste. It is because of the inner life force that the outer shell can move with action. We wouldn't move our body if we didn't think to move, or feel like moving, or want to express or do something.

Now, that which is the essence of life which came from the original life Source is our spirit. Without the spirit, we would not become a movable, living sentient entity. What remains without the spirit of life is a form which is not moving with life. The farther one strays from the original essence of the Spirit of Life, the quality and strength of the life energy will diminish from the material fiber. This would inflict the world with destructive energy because it is polarized from sustainable life energy. It's an undoing or a corruption of the *creative* energy. Remember, the polarization process didn't occur until Creation began. God is a perfection of life energy which is eternal. The closer one stays connected with the original Spirit of Life, the stronger is the purity of the life force within the material fiber and it reflects an image or reflection of a divine personality. All life originated from the divine energy - the will of the Creator to share and flow forth with loving energy.

This life giving energy radiated out into diverse expressions of life, just as the sun's rays radiate light energy. The light doesn't just reflect light for sight. It also reflects the essence of molecular particles into diverse combinations which give life to particles of cells. Each cell then multiplies and forms its own unique organ, an essential part of the whole body of interconnected organs.

Each organ has that which is seen and that which is unseen. Our existence needs to incorporate the matrices of life in some parallel manifestation. We have a physical nose for the purpose to enable our body to smell and breathe air (invisible matrix) in and out. The brain is a physical organ, while the mind is the invisible matrix for thought, (the beginning of will). Eyes are the organs for the essence of sight, etc. Our body is the physical makeup of multiple organs, while our soul is the unseen vessel for a specific being of life. The three matrices are: air (breath), water (our body consists of 3/4 water), and fire (the eyes and mind reflect light). We have will power and the life force (spirit) to enable us to move with action.

All of these expressions branch into other dimensions of biology, math, psychology, emotions, art, music, etc. They all reflect the nature of God's invisible attributes.

Dimension of Arts and Nature

I found the intricate dimensions within dimensions complicated to explain because of my limited knowledge of diverse subjects. The spiritual images flowed extremely quick - much faster than my brain could take in all at once. Each expression built upon each other, while they all reflected a part of God's invisible essence. When I thought about the dimensions, my mind divided into an array within the dimensions and I could not fathom anything further until the basic foundation that I had learned was secure. This is why experts specialize in one particular major area while minoring in other areas. They may have knowledge in multiple areas, but not as in-depth as the subject they specialize. Who could fathom complete knowledge in all professions? We were each given our own particular talents and area of expertise because the totality of omniscience was incomprehensible for us to understand all at once. Each of us had to specialize in our own area. Our individual focus should never diminish the importance of diverse knowledge in other areas.

All at the same time, I perceived the interlinking and interchanging attributes of art, math, language, science, biology, astronomy, music, etc. Art begins with the value of black and white (night/day, unseen/seen, unknown/known). Then there are the three basic colors with a property of light: yellow, blue, and red -- just as the primary beginning matrices are air (yellow), water (blue), and fire (red). Then there are new colors which are formed from combinations of different amounts of these colors. There are secondary colors (from blending the primary colors), and complementary colors (the opposite of the primary colors). There are analogous, monochromatic, contrasting colors, etc. into an infinite array of diverse colors.

Mathematics begin with a point and then it branches out with positive and negative dimensions as addition and subtraction. A single

Dimensions of Creation

point becomes two dimensional with length and width and expands into triangles, squares, circles, etc. and then multiplies into an infinite plane surface. This surface then radiated into three dimensional forms (width, length and height) of diverse shapes (cone, cylinder, cube, globe, etc.). Infinite numbers radiated out and expressed multiplication, reflecting sizes (proportion) and shapes. Then there are the complimentary mathematical attributes, such as definite equations, subtraction and division.

Language begins with letters (sounds) which combine together to form words, which in turn forms simple sentences of subject and predicate, like: *'I am'* or *'She laughed'*. There are words which mean the same, and words which have opposite definitions. There are synonyms, antonyms, and homonyms, etc. Words combine to form sentences and multiple sentences compose a story. Everything builds upon parallel building blocks.

Biology studies life and living matter. There is an analogous relationship in the makeup of plants, animals, and insects. Cells divide and multiply, and interact differently with different genes of DNA, molecules, and properties. Water and oil does not mix, while other liquids have no difficulty mixing and forming new products through diverse properties, etc.

If we look at each area of study, we can see that they have the same properties that govern them. They all reflect the natural law of life which is diverse with an order of harmony that grows and expands, or shrinks and lessens. Our lungs even expand and contract with air as we breathe.

I'm not an expert in any of these fields, but I can see a relationship within each category. Now expand this into the dimension of man. We are all related and founded upon the spiritual characteristics of God. We are each unique in various ways and yet we are all human. One group of people is not more important than another group. Would we say that math is more important than biology or language, etc.? What would we do if any one of these did not exist? Without language, we couldn't communicate, and without math we couldn't calculate or build. Without science we couldn't discover the nature of things. Without art or music, we couldn't express our emotions with beauty, color or sound. Life is a connection of diverse things which brings beauty and expression through harmony and unity as well as chaos and division.

All characteristics and forms of life are important and we are all related. We <u>all</u> came from the same universal Source which gave us life. People are characterized into diverse differences, but that doesn't place any group higher in importance than any other. Do you wonder why God used a bow in the sky as a sign to Noah? The rainbow suffused different colors into a relationship with its neighbor, while each of the colors also independently expresses its own individual beauty. They co-exist side by side in harmony.

Like the rainbow, each person has unique, individual characteristics which expresses our individuality and beauty. We live side by side with diverse populations of people. We can live in harmony with one another if we try, if we really want to live in peace. It's a matter of our collective will which starts with the intentions of the heart. Wouldn't our world reflect a gorgeous rainbow if we joined our hearts together in love! If only we would choose to reject the friction that pulls us away from each other. That friction comes from the arrogance of superior attitudes and ignorance of the beauty of human diversity. Too many of us try to destroy the individual beauty of the human expression instead of appreciating each other for who we are.

What would our world be like if we destroyed just one primary color of the rainbow? If we destroyed blue, then we couldn't see all of the richness of the depth of the blue sky and the ocean as we do now. We wouldn't see the colors which expand into hues of green and purple either. Our world would be less expressive and less colorful. That one primary color is important to bring infinite colors into our world. Why should we restrain life from expressing itself with diverse beauty when life itself was created for that specific purpose?

Take this concept a step further and reason what would happen to our world without one of the beginning foundations of life. Everything on earth needs water, oxygen and light. What if water, or oxygen or light was destroyed? All of life would cease to exist! All things in life have a reason and a purpose to exist. If there were no purpose, then it wouldn't exist in the first place.

People also need to express our emotions through song and prayer. When the heart is happy, there is song and praise and we feel uplifted with positive, rejuvenating energy. Human nature needs to learn to balance and harmonize with our universe. Music is a way for self expression of the heart. Music has a blend of harmony and tranquility with softness, and also has a contrast of loud, vibrant sound, but it still composes an ensemble of harmonies to form a soothing song. Different instruments are needed to bring a variety of sounds into a masterpiece. The perfect blend of notes, rhythm, and emotion will join together with a balance of composition. Diverse musical instruments sound beautiful when they are in harmony with one another, but when one instrument is out of tune, then the whole composition is out of sync or sounds abrasive.

This is why we need to be cautious of the type of energy we express through our actions. Energy is the source of life. We can use it for good or to do harm. We learn through both expressions. But while positive energy gives birth to blessings, negative energy destroys.

If we could picture all of creation as a giant jigsaw puzzle, we could understand that one missing piece from the complete puzzle ruins the picture. God doesn't want to have any holes in His picture of Creation. We all fit back together in harmony if we will only try to live with the energy of love in our hearts. This is an impossible task without understanding where we're heading. This is why I received all of this information. I was chosen to share what I received from the spirit of the Living Universe. God is love, and when we join hands together in love, then God will graft us back together as one in harmony, to form the perfect portrait of alliance. This is why the rainbow was given as a sign to Noah. The rainbow is a symbolic covenant to remind us to express ourselves by reflecting the harmony of the universe. We must come together, united side by side as equal partners. We must be united in our hearts with positive expressions of love to reflect a world of beauty and peace.

Can you see how there are lessons in all things ... and life never ends! Life on earth is what we collectively make it. I am hoping that with better spiritual insight of how our world operates, that we can make better informed decisions for our future.

The information which I received in the spirit (and amazingly all in just one week!) is more precious to me than my very own life. I know deep within my heart that our world can be transformed by the renewing of our heart with a universal restoration of the spirit. I was driven solely by a deeper understanding in union with the Holy Spirit to try my best to articulate in words that which I received through visions and divine revelation. I hope and pray that I was able to deliver the message as clearly as needed to help our world. It is my hope for all humanity to be raised up in a clearer directive of our highest goals - to live in peace with one another and to discover the beauty of life as it was meant to be. The wisdom of God to create with diversity is so utterly amazing! There's so much to explore and enjoy in a world as awesome as we were given. It has everything we need if we honor and respect its sacredness.

Chapter Six
Creation

On the seventh day of Creation God rested; not that creation was complete, but a pause, to reflect. All was good and done except completeness. God had finished Creation up to the point of a divine purpose and plan. Now it is the responsibility of each soul to complete their own destiny -- to become what they focused their energy and will on to find their place within the all.

God is eternal and unfathomable and must reveal this essence of infinite 'continuance' for created beings to have eternal life, because *Creation reflects as a mirror God's own attributes*. Should God stop revealing divine attributes, Creation would have an end of learning and of evolving toward divine knowledge. Through this mirroring process immortality is reflected and made possible for created beings. A reflection is like a mirror and so God created an image of God's likeness. Unto this likeness God created all things through it and for it. What was missing from creation's completeness? . . . To be known. God wants to be loved and known. Likewise, each person has a drive within their self to be loved and to express their self as who they are. For God to be known, there had to be a way to reveal and enlighten us to evolve into our highest potential.

God is all-in-all, self-sufficient and does not need anything or anyone for sustenance. But God wanted to express love and so wanted another to receive this love and share all that divinity is. And so, God paused to reflect on the revealing of God's eternal existence. God needed something to reveal to (which is Creation) and something through which to reveal to the unknowledgeable realm to evolve into the knowledgeable realm (the Revealer is the Holy Spirit). And because God did not complete revealing to Creation, they were given knowledge through infinite ways. We were given the opportunity to find and learn of God if we would open ourselves up as clean vessels so we could reflect divine attributes in purity.

The commandment that we rest on the Sabbath is to reflect (think about) God and aspire to emulate perfection. We worship God to acknowledge God's perfection. When we seek to understand God's greatness then we admire all that God is and we try to improve ourselves. I understand that God is pleased that we seek God's ways because in doing so, we are respecting and honoring all life. I felt that God wants to have a communion with each and every one of us, but only does so when we are willing to be a living vessel which graciously accepts the indwelling Holy Spirit. It can't dwell within us if we are in enmity with the pure spirit. When we prepare our spirit to reflect goodness and love, we are becoming a compatible vessel for God to disclose divine things to us.

At first we receive revelations by little increments at a time because divine wisdom is too overwhelming for us to understand all at once. It's as telling a newborn baby to fly an airplane. The baby first needs to grow in physical capabilities and intellectual maturity before he may fly an airplane. So it is for all people to begin with the tiny steps before we may be ready for the more advanced spiritual things. A drop of divine revelation is as an ocean-worth of transcended vision. We can't hold it all at once. Thus obtaining divine knowledge is a never-ending process of discovery.

God only needs to say, *"Let there be,"* and it is so, but God *chose* to create with an order. God chose for Creation to have freedom to choose to have a relationship with God and so gave us the free will to choose our destiny. Love isn't pure if it is forced upon us. God wanted us to choose to love our Creator by our free will. God sends revelations to those who lovingly seek and sincerely <u>desire</u> to find our Source.

When we stop turning toward our Creator of life and eternity, then we may be in danger of turning away into its polarity. We then fall down toward the destruction of life and toward mortality. For the sustenance of life, we must turn toward God so we may absorb divine light as the sunlight is absorbed by plants through photosynthesis. As plants grow, so do we evolve in divine wisdom and likeness. As God sends revelations, we need to reflect on what God reveals to us. Those who truly worship God keep life evolving for all of us just as God rains down on all. God's creation will continue to evolve because God is infinite. God is not totally ever known in completeness in the physical realm and this is why God is unfathomable for us. Because infinity has no end, there can be no end to divine revelations, otherwise we would not continue to evolve in divine knowledge to reflect God's ways.

To stifle the freedom to learn is to imprison our mind and to thwart further evolution of knowledge. When people block or reject spiritual revelation, they are limiting and rejecting God's intervention to help us. Sooner or later their misconceptions will fall away because truth will be known.

The creation of humankind began with God's concealment to the lower human level, which became part of the darkness because God was unseen/unknown. Light was also created because in the darkness, light (revelation) is seen and God becomes known according to what is revealed to us.

God is perfect and without sin. It was this *process* to give creation eternal life, (because God wanted us to live forever), and for God 'to be known' which gave beginning to our lack of knowledge. Ignorance is a product of the beginning process to begin our spiritual and intellectual growth, but through ignorance comes error and sin. Sin was not reflected into Creation in the beginning process but through our ignorance, it was inevitable. When sin appears, there begins a parting. Sin is a defective path which divides us from divine perfection and hinders us from the Light.

Sin's development is the mystery of unfathomableness in which we have difficulty in understanding why it was necessary. Through my divine revelation, I understand why sin must appear although I find it difficult to explain. Please bare with me as I am struggling to put this into words. In perfect wisdom, God knew that if knowledge would be held back, then sin would appear, but it was more important to make our life eternal for those who evolve in perfection. And so God reflected whether to have this happen.

If God chose not to permit sin to appear then through logic and order, Creation would be mortal because it wouldn't reflect infinity through God's continual unveiling. What a problem. God wants to be known by Creation; but, to complete Creation during this mirroring process would result with an end to our life and all manifested things. That would not correctly reflect God's essence as eternal, therefore we would not be eternal beings. God found a way to reflect the divine attribute of eternity by pausing or holding back an end of finishing creation by permitting a continual evolution of revealing to us through revelations and through nature. And so, God's reflection of eternity had to include sin's appearance because we were not all-knowing.

God didn't like sin nor had sin, and so turned away from its manifestation. Likewise God does not pour out revelation to sinful people because they are not able to understand it. God patiently awaits for us to spiritually mature until we are able to understand the light and embrace divine truth. The key is our willingness to embrace and accept it.

When man turns away from God, there is a separation, a disconnect. This begins the illusion of separation from God just as darkness separates from light; of not knowing and knowing; of not seeing and seeing; of negative and positive energy, etc. into their dimensions. This is the reason creation has sin in its existence. The world was created with logic and an order of complimentary forces. The opposite of knowledge is ignorance. God didn't want to give us any form of affliction or problems although it is through sin that pain, opposition, suffering, conflict, etc. occurs in their dimensions. Through this polarization of forces, everything would have a cause and effect, and a sense of divine order. The farther we fall away from righteousness would cause negative consequences, which God wanted to use to help steer us back on track. It is natural for people to want to avoid pain and negative consequences. It was God's hope that we would learn from the consequences of our mistakes so that we would turn back to the light and receive healing.

God spent a long process of analyzing whether to permit sin's manifestation in order to give eternity to Creation. God foresaw a plan to use the consequences of sin and the polarization process to discipline Creation and would wait patiently for our life experiences to develop our character. If the natural unfolding of consequences did not steer us back on track and we still continued to fall away, then God would present different ways to interact with us to help steer us back along the path of goodness but without removing our free will. God was prepared to interact with incrementing degrees of power according to the situation. God was very conscious of not wanting to force us against our will and yet didn't want us to fall astray into constant darkness. God was very adamant in permitting our own freedom of choice to guide our development through life lessons, although still wanted us to choose the path of righteousness so that we would not have to suffer. But that is our choice.

Since we are not all-knowing, then we make choices through our ignorance. This made it necessary for God to send divine guidance to initiate our growth, except there was no one who had a mature clean vessel that was able to hold divine revelations yet. Therefore God sent angels and archangels who could hold God's messages, to deliver guidance to certain people who would share with the people. These were the prophets who were given authority to deliver divine guidance to the people who were not able to connect with God yet. The guidance that was delivered to us through prophets was to encourage each of us to seek a personal spiritual connection with God so that we may obtain knowledge through the Holy Spirit. How were we to seek God if we were not even aware that such a connection was available to us?

Everything manifested in our world is known by the truth of its existence. Wisdom yet unknown or undisclosed in our realm can be revealed or realized if it is founded upon the truth. In this way scientists and philosophers discover many new discoveries because they may find supporting evidence through nature and through empirical means. They may see the cycle of seasons, the transformations of life, the renewing of life through healing, etc. The mysterious spark of life that resides in all of us is yet to be understood. That's why God chose to create with a logical order. God wants us to discover, learn and evolve in the things which are seen as well as the things which are unseen.

In regards to the unseen, people need to evoke God to pour out divine wisdom and then we may testify to the truth to enlighten others to discover things from the spiritual realm and be realized on earth - "on earth as it is in Heaven". In this way, ignorance is overcome because truth and knowledge is revealed, seen, experienced and understood. It is our responsibility to shine the light.

This is why God provides guidance so that we would not have to stay in darkness and yet it is still our choice. If we don't arise in knowledge, then we remain at risk of wallowing in darkness or semi darkness. We suffer at the hands of our own wrongdoing which causes hardships and harsh consequences through ill will, oppression of our freedom and negative deeds. God wanted to guide and shield us from the pains of wrongdoing and so sent guidance as an opportunity to lead us into knowledge if we believed and followed the upright path. If we lived upright lives and turned to God, then we would live closer in heart to God and blessings would flow from above. When we live in sin, we are the farthest away from God and we defile our character, (which in turn is detrimental to our society and world).

Our social interactions and customs reflect the qualities that we choose to follow, (or are forced upon us through oppression). We need to be careful not to fall away into the dimension of self absorption. The opposite of looking toward God is looking away from God. Not looking toward God is looking toward self because these are reciprocal. For example, it's not that having wealth is causing people to be greedy or less compassionate, but what matters is what we choose to focus our energy on. What we do with it, and how it effects our heart and of course our action is the key. The stronger we become self-absorbed, the more we do things which are detrimental to society because we think more about ourself than anyone or anything else. The human side of being **overly** self-absorbed includes the qualities of selfishness, greed, arrogance, aggression, extreme hedonism, oppression, impurity, crimes that are self serving and causes injustice to others, etc. So we need to keep our heart in check.

The reciprocal human qualities which emulate divine qualities include: generosity, charity, respect, meekness, empathy, philanthropy, purity, service, justice, etc. There are wealthy people who contribute a lot of their money to charity and research to benefit our world. Again, wealth is not what causes some people to become greedy or less compassionate. It's what people choose to focus their energy on - "oneself or all". Do they place themselves as being the most important, or will they consider the greater all?

Since God reflects everywhere, inside and out, God's invisible attributes can be found inside ourselves when we live a just, upright life. The heart symbolizes our love. If we give our love to God, we have a connection to God and our love benefits all. If we give our devotion to a self-serving life, then our lives become tainted, deceitful, harmful and unjust toward others, then we go astray and we will fall farther away from divine attributes and plummet into sin. The lives of those who fall into sin want to do harmful things to one another which brings them into ruin.

God accomplished much thinking and creating in each of the six days. (Days are from God's perspective because time doesn't exist in the spirit realm as we know it. Time and space were manifested with creation). God was as busy and as thorough on the seventh day as on all the six previous days except our ending was not finalized. In place of finishing Creation on the seventh day, God paused and waited on us to decide our destiny.

God does not tire; if God were to stop, then all creation would stop. As God reflected divine goodness within Creation, God wanted us to reciprocate and choose to reflect goodness through our thoughts and actions. As a covenant, we were guided to keep the Sabbath day holy (clean), to make an extra effort to do good deeds and to be mindful of what we do.

When we make mistakes, we need to acknowledge and identify the error. When the error is identified, we then need to improve and reform our ways to do what is upright. Divine guidance was given to us through the

Servants of God (those to whom the Divine Creator chooses to deliver a divine message) in order to help guide our behavior back on track. We are forgiven when we turn back to God (repent), but we fall astray into sin when we continue away (intentionally or unintentional). Intentional sin is really only deeper into ignorance, for if you had total knowledge, you would not sin. Sin is not of God but if we knew the Truth then there is hope to combat ignorance. There exists a chance of revelation and turning back to God. This revealing is the hope in continuing on a path of righteousness and the reason why God chose prophets and messengers to inform humankind to seek divine guidance.

God wanted to reveal knowledge to us in an intermitting sequence and in gradual amounts that we could handle. People had to feel, touch, and experience all things to learn. When we obtain knowledge through divine revelations, we can understand more fully our destiny and can ascend back toward God. People have a job to overcome ignorance. Creation began in a temporary state of 'not knowing' so that God could reveal knowledge while having a communion with those who sincerely seek to find God. This began the dimension of learning infinite possibilities. *"For all that may be known of God by men lies plain before their eye; indeed God himself has disclosed it to them. His invisible attributes, that is to say his everlasting power and deity, have been visible, ever since the world began, to the eye of reason, in the things he has made."*[17]

We cannot hold *all* knowledge at once because there isn't an end to knowledge. We cannot know all things or there would be a stopping point for wisdom. This is why each of us have different interests, skills and knowledge about diverse subjects. Each of us contributes our unique area of expertise while knowledge continues to expand.

All that there is to know is collectively known only by God. God is like an ocean where all the waters are rejoined. The wisdom of each and every human, and each and every creature is instantly transmitted to God. There is nothing that God does not know.

Chapter Seven

The Living Mirror

Look into a mirror in a darkened room and light a match in front of the mirror. The match is the source of light used to reveal yourself. Without the match, you are shrouded in darkness and cannot see yourself in the mirror and yet you are there. You know that you exist even though you can't see yourself in the darkness. While the light reflects your image into the mirror, the image in the mirror is not you, but a likeness. The reflection in the mirror of the lit match is not the beginning source of its light. The match is the true fire while its reflection in the mirror is a copy, like the sun reflects its light onto the moon.

Now, place a mirror facing the mirror on the opposite side of the match. The light reflects into infinity within the mirrors. The match is the true source of light, but if we ignore the real match and only focus on its reflection, we are fooled about which is the origin. When we focus on the real match, we see the truth of the true source without illusion.

For God to hold back final revelation of God's entirety through this "mirroring" process, God's wholeness was concealed between the two mirrors and only reflected invisible essences in order to give Creation eternity. *"And Moses prayed, 'Show me thy glory.' The Lord answered, 'I will make all my goodness (character) pass before you.'* (*Exodus 33:18-19*) *'My face you cannot see, for no <u>mortal</u> man may see me and live.' The Lord said, 'Here is a place beside me. Take your stand on the rock and when my glory passes by, I will put you in a crevice of the rock and cover you with my* *hand until I have passed by. Then I will take away my hand, and you shall see my back, but my face shall not be seen.'* (Exodus 33:21-23)

As a symbol of the above scripture, Moses was placed in the crevice of the rock to reflect God's revealing between the mirrors, and the hand concealed God's fullness of identity just as our minds are veiled from knowing all things. If mortal man were to see God completely within our dimension in the flesh, they would likely die because God's fullness of immortality would end the essence of 'continuation' in the *Living Mirror* of this physical realm. Finality would have been conveyed to Moses during the mirroring process, thereby removing the essence of immortality to humankind. (But the spirit realm is different.)

God always was and always will be, but Creation needed evidence of this to combat ignorance. God reveals insight to humans drop by drop by showing parts of divinity through the mirrors. The more Creation sees of it's fullness, the more knowledge they will have of God (and of themselves and of all things because Creation reflects God). *"Now we see only puzzling reflections in a mirror, but then we shall see face to face. My knowledge now is partial; then it will be whole, like God's knowledge of me."*[18] One day our knowledge of God will be whole, but only at the proper time and the proper realm.

This is also one of the significant meanings of the two angels on top of the Ark of the Covenant. The two angels are representing the eternal male/female spiritual reflections of the dimensions of the upper and lower (seen and unseen) Creation, while reflecting each other. They face each other and God's essence is revealed from the light of the Holy Spirit between them.

Also paralleling this meaning are the two mirrors which are the two waters that reflect each other as told in Genesis.[19] When the water ripples, there is distortion and so error begins. When the water calms there is a clearer image revealed. When truth is revealed, its light radiates throughout the depths of everything just as the match is seen repeatedly within the two mirrors which are facing each other. This is why we are the light of the world and we are to let our light shine (reflect and reveal). We are not to hide our light under a bushel, but set it on top of a stand (foundation) for all to see.

When we learn, we are growing and expanding in wisdom. God is not confined, but is free and unlimited. Truth is not confined, but it is free to learn. This is why God is unfathomable. Those who say that their religion is complete within their book of scripture alone are in error. No religion is complete until the worshipers learn <u>through the spirit</u> and discover God through a personal divine communion. Isaiah 64:1 says, *"I was there to be sought by a people who did not ask, to be found by men who did not seek me."*

God reveals to true seekers in spirit. This is the way of God and the nature of our existence. Worship wasn't intended for people to just go to a sanctuary to listen to a man dictate dogma. It was meant to look for God wherever you are and reflect to find a communion with God. The word *Worship* should immediately remind you of God, not a material building. The next time someone asks you, *"Where do you worship God?"* your answer should be, "<u>in your heart</u>". All people may worship God in their heart. Every human has a heart. The heart is universal and does not ostracize or cut off anyone from worship. God is available to all people, without discrimination. When we truly desire to seek God, then our prayers, meditations, songs, etc. radiate upwards from our heart. A heart filled with love connects us to God and to life.

The true way to worship God is to seek and emulate divine ways. Keep the Sabbath holy; that's why we were given this covenant, although some people do not understand what it means to keep the Sabbath holy.

Holy means clean and pure; not artificial or fake. Keep your heart clean and pure. The cleaner your devotion and attention is given to God, the clearer the reflection will be to open up the line of communion to receive revelations from God. God searches our hearts and reveals to us only what we can handle and according to God's perfect plan.

In all the words that I am using to try to share with you now, I realize that there is still some room for misunderstandings. Though I speak in truth by trying to reciprocate what I had received and witnessed from the spirit, those receiving my words if not attuned to God, may not understand my words in their true intention. It is very common for people to misunderstand our true intentions. This is why each of us are responsible to turn to God to find understanding. Also, the revelations that I had received are only droplets from the ocean. There is no end to revelations. There is always more to learn. No one person can know all the answers; only God is omniscient. God's messengers can only share that part of what God reveals to them in hopes to inspire others to seek for themselves.

When humankind generally slows down its pace of learning, then God sends revelations to whomever is chosen to receive them and to share with others. I can feel through the revelations that I received that humanity needs to spiritually expand because as a whole, we had become spiritually stagnant. I feel that I am insignificant to this world, no one of importance or notoriety and yet the message that I received is important to help all of humanity. I'm trying to overcome my insecurities about my humaness even though I am truly shocked that God should choose me to be a witness to divine truth. But then again, I am sad that God could not find many others in abundance who are also ready to accept divine revelations. Any person is capable of obtaining enlightenment, but it is an ongoing process of spiritual evolution of which an open heart is a must.

This world holds fast to deceit but it's because they don't know any better. Now and again, God intervenes with people to nudge us forward. The only way to overcome misconceptions about the spirit is through spiritual evidence. This evidence is difficult for people to accept when it confronts our established beliefs brought about through human interpretations of religious dogma. God gave all nations helpful guidance through revelation and it is in written form (given through messengers) so that we would have something to help us recognize the truth and yet scripture continues to be misunderstood by people in many different ways.

    I am aware of the imperfections I contain so please don't assume that I am perfect. It is not the *imperfections* that keep people away from God, but it is the *action* of either growing toward or away that moves us to being either closer or farther from God. The closer I am drawn toward God's invisible attributes in the spirit, the more I may reflect this in my "essence". Of course, needless to say, I nor anyone else can be God because we were created as an individual human entity, but some of God's attributes can be seen and recognized within each of us in degrees of clarity. Don't deny the divinity within you. Doing so is denying that God is divine, for where else did you originate if not from God? You were created as a powerful and capable human being. You are worthy.

    People reflect a distorted or cloudy likeness of God's attributes. Our goal is to choose to reflect a clean, transparent likeness of divine attributes without blemish. If anyone could arise and obtain as close as possible toward perfection, they would contain God's very reflection,[20] like Christ reflects God's essence. Those who emulate the Christ likeness within are in harmony and unison with divinity. Christ is not a name, but a state of being. The highest goal of humanity is to obtain Christhood which clearly reflects divine attributes. When we are not aware of our own divinity within, we may not even attempt to emulate divinity because we don't know that it's possible. Each of us has the capacity to be magnificent, excellent humans who emulate divinity.

The word Christ comes from the Greek word *khristos* which means "the annointed". Khristos is equivalent to the Hebrew word *mashiah* "messiah", or the Aramaic word *meshiha*, or the Greek word *messias* which means "anoint". The word Messiah or Christ is actually a title depicting Jesus' Christhood. Jesus the Christ was in the state of khristos because he reflected a clean image of God's spiritual attributes[21] in human form. Jesus was full of the Holy Spirit; full of God's light. God our Creator shined fully and brightly within Jesus.

Likewise, when any human ascends in righteousness, they reflect a clearer image of God's holy attributes. It is these who are called by God as spiritual Children. If people will heed the examples of those who have attained the khristos and became incorporated with the same Holy Spirit, then they are also following God because they become one in spirit.[22]

"So God created man in His own image" [God used His reflection in the Living Mirror to create man]; *"in the image of God"* [in the khristos image], *"he created him"* [the khristos likeness, namely humankind]; *"male and female he created them" [the masculine and the feminine, man and woman].*[23] God used the khristos image to create life forms. His Son is reflected with God because the khristos is in God and then reflected in and throughout the infinite creation.[24]

The highest level that man could ever ascend is to the reflection of God's likeness, which is God's spiritual Son.[25] Humankind is imperfect compared to God's perfection and it's very difficult to obtain the reflection of the Son and yet this is God's goal for all humanity. Jesus was a living example for us to <u>follow</u>. God wants us to become a clean vessel that rises upward in spiritual union of the enlightened one just as Jesus and others had attained.

Different religions use different words describing this same concept of the annointed or enlightened one, (although I don't believe that all people within a religious community of any brand of religion understand the full extent as it was divinely intended to mean). We all have words which symbolize the same standards of the spirit: Christ the annointed, the Buddhist bodhi, the Hindu Sannyasis, Muslim Caliph, Jewish Tzedek, and possibly the Chi flow with the Kundalini awakening, etc. Our goal is to emulate the people who have obtained the khristos. That is why God searches our hearts and whole being. God inspires and watches over those who aspire to follow the upper path of goodness and righteousness. It's not the name of our religion which justifies us, but the inner spirit of our heart which defines who we are in God's eyes.

So, if you choose to emulate divinity, then choose God as your highest longing to know. Contemplate on God and the mystery through scripture. Seek the good things throughout Creation and come to know goodness within yourself. Avoid doing harm to anyone. Learn until the Word becomes a Living Word in you! Another person cannot do the searching for you. You can't rely on another person to find the khristos for you. They may share their discoveries with you just as I am doing here, but ultimately you have to take it upon yourself to personally seek God. When your heart is trained and ready to receive divine revelations, then the Holy Spirit will come upon you and will give you divine insights. And when you receive these divine revelations, you will be in awe beyond anything you've ever felt before. I can't stress enough how important it is to prepare yourself for this annointing. It takes such a long time for humankind to accomplish, especially if we were brainwashed to believe that it couldn't happen.

When I apply my mind to reflect about what I was shown through revelations and visions, I compared them with the scriptures and testimonies of others. In this way, the scriptures came alive with deeper and more personal insights of understanding. I also found a richer understanding by reading scripture from other religions as well. I saw parallels and unity of what I and others have tried to testify in their own words of what was revealed to each of us. I see the same truth expressed in different ways of stating the same thing throughout various religions. Each religion is only a facet of what various people perceived from God's revelations. As knowledge is infinite, there are many drops of revelation needed to be understood with more clarity. All faiths are all interconnected by numerous interpretations of divine information raining down from the same Source. It is difficult to explain something which is beyond our comprehension without direct revelations from God. I don't think that I would have ever progressed to this level of consciousness if the revelations were interpreted second-hand from another human.

Chapter Eight
The Mystery of Christ Revealed

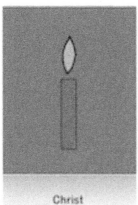 

Christ
Spiritual Living "Mirror" which reflects an invisible image of God. This represents a state of union with the Holy Spirit.

Holy Spirit
True Light from God

*Note
You cannot see God in the Living Mirror because this is concealed. The essence of divinity is reflected through the Christ mirror. The Holy Spirit shines God's invisible attributes into Christ.

"The Trinity" - illustration by Sandy Briggs

Shine The Light

Original candle (True Light) - Photo by Sandy Briggs

In the Jewish texts, they give acknowledgment to the three beginning matrices or 'mothers' which came from God which is: air, water and fire; 'alef', 'mem' and 'shin', respectively. These are the first elements which God used to give birth to everything else thereafter. Although I do want to point out that these are also symbolic for what God has given me to explain. For a lack of better words, these are what the human mind understands through language. In the diagram above, the candle represents the fire, the area around the candle is the air, and the mirror represents the water. Water reflects like a mirror, and this becomes a multi-faceted feature which resonates throughout Creation. But I will get to that later.

Light Source and its reflection - Photo by Sandy Briggs

Before these three *'mothers'*, there is the One true Source/Creator who is everything that is reflected throughout Creation. Then there is that to whom the Source reveals (which is the Creation), and the one who does the illuminating (the Holy Spirit). These are parallel with the Trinity of the Father, Son and Holy Ghost analogy. No one can be The Creator Father except the One and only True Source of all life. The Son is a reflection of God's attributes as demonstrated in the photo above as the reflection of the candle is reflected through the mirror. We cannot be the Holy Spirit, but the Holy Spirit can be in us.

The khristos (Christhood), is the first state of a clear reflection; as an original thing is reflected as a duplicate image within a mirror. This mirrored image has a beginning without blemish or distortion although this image has always been within God because it *is* God's reflection. It is as light from light. Mother Father God had no beginning because this Conscious Source has always existed even before choosing to create life forms. This is complicated to our mind and yet it is simple when God reveals to us and fills us with understanding. I am in awe of this information and I hope that I am helping to clarify it with better understanding so that others may be encouraged to seek your own drops of

Shine The Light

divine wisdom. When God reveals knowledge, then ignorance is dissolved and I know that there is so much more to be disclosed.

Now if God should choose to entirely reveal everything to us through this process, then it is my understanding that all knowledge, etc. would be revealed all at once but we would shatter. This would be wonderful for God to entirely reveal everything to us so that error stops and sin is conquered, but the only problem is that people cannot contain infinite knowledge in our mortal state. We can only handle limited, specialized areas of knowledge. We learn by increments as we grow and mature in understanding, like building blocks.

Distorted reflection - Photo by Sandy Briggs

The Mystery of Christ Revealed

Our dilemma is that knowledge is stunted because of our stubbornness to stick with old misconceptions and rejecting any corrections or deeper insights into our established belief. The farther our belief strays away from the truth lessens the light or "clouds our mirror" which prevents us from receiving new revelations because we can't *see*. Our mind's ability to reflect becomes dull and cloudy, like stagnant water, preventing the light to enter. Therefore, we must continually cleanse and prepare ourselves to become clearer spiritual vessels which enables us to see higher truth more clearly.

One lifetime is not long enough for any of us to learn all that there is to learn. Omniscience is too powerful and too vast to be confined within a limited human mind. Just as we grow and expand our physical body, so do we need to expand in the spirit. If God were to fill us with more than we could handle all at once, then our 'skins' would burst. Does this remind you of the story Jesus told about the wine skins? He explained that new wine must be poured into new wine skins because old skins will burst. This is also why people cannot see God's entire true essence on earth and live. But when our spiritual body reaches and sees into the spiritual realm, then there are no limits in the spirit. People can see God in the Spirit (if God wishes it to be so), because the spiritual body is free and immortal.

On earth, God can send representatives so that we may learn of God, just as God was represented by angels and messengers, or as the burning bush, cloud, and pillar of fire which Moses saw.

During my near-death experience, in which I shared in my first book, I truly was able to see God the Father in the Spirit realm, and yet I still could only understand Him in increments of disclosure. There was no danger of bursting in the Spirit realm of light. But after I received this huge download of spiritual insight, I can now understand why God always has to

Shine The Light

conceal something from us, such as Mother God in my case, for eternal revelations to continue.

Introduction of second mirror - Photo by Sandy Briggs

This should help us better understand the following scripture: *"Man is the image of God, and the mirror of his glory, whereas women reflects the glory of man."*[26] God took a piece from the Living Mirror (a rib from Adam's side) to have another 'mirror', like breaking the mirror into two pieces. God made the image of Man male and female[27] by placing each mirror on the opposite side of the candle light at the proper angle. The Divine Consciousness revealed the masculine hemisphere's character through the mirror to the first man. At the same time, revealing the feminine hemisphere's character through the second mirror to the first woman.[28] The woman in her purest state reflects an invisible likeness of divinity's attributes within herself along with the reflection of the first mirror's image (man), through the light of the Holy Spirit.

The woman is of equal value as a 'mirror', for now man reflects woman, and woman reflects man through the two mirrors. *"In Christ's fellowship woman is as essential to man as man to woman."*[29] This is also why some men have more feminine characteristics than others, and why some women have more masculine characteristics than other women. Women and men are shown different hemispheres of divinity from the same Source while still reflecting each other. (A feminine image was created after the masculine image, but they are equal in God's eyes.)

In Egyptian hieroglyphics, there is an eye as a symbol which depicts this. (Remember, Moses was trained in the ways of the Egyptians.) In the Jewish text Kabbalah, it explains the 'ayin' (eye), and the 'ain', which is the profile of half a face called the macroprosopus. If you research deeply, you will find evidence of this explanation above. There are already books explaining this concept which get pretty in-depth. Therefore, I am not being inspired to expand upon this further for you. Likewise, this book is not intended to answer all of your questions, but to encourage people to look for answers that have already been shared in other books of antiquity. I am not bringing any new concepts to the world that wasn't already explained somewhere else. As it says in the Bible: *"For all the ancient scriptures were written for our own instruction."*[30] and: *"the use of books is endless, and much study is wearisome."*[31] This scripture encourages all people to study all of the ancient scriptures and books thus acknowledging that we should not be confined to just one book. It also reminds us that such study is vast. But through study, we will grow in understanding when we apply our mind to reason. The goal is to come together with tolerance and understanding of the vastness of truth which is shared in the universal commonalities among us all. We then should see beyond the ignorance of bigotry and prejudice which has lead us to needless war and oppression. In this way, we should come to our senses and strive to drop our weapons and make peace with one another.

Original candle with reflections of the original male
and female reflections, and male and female children -
Photo by Sandy Briggs

Woman, (the second mirror) was given the essence of reproducing children (male and female), as a reflection of the replicating images within the mirrors. One mirror cannot reflect copies within itself without the duplicating process which is enabled by the second mirror. The woman may produce a number of offspring just as the mirrors reflect dimensions of likenesses within itself, but she needs the male counterpart's seed in order to use its DNA in this material world. Just as the mirror reflects infinite dimensions within two mirrors facing each other, so does the chromosomes of the egg and sperm multiply when they come together. This is the spark of a *living* reflection.

We may only assist God in co-creating. A woman cannot give birth to a child of just her own doing without the help of her counter male partner's sperm and God's power to send the spirit to give it life. We only have the abilities that God gives to us. God can enable humans to give birth to a baby from the union of a male sperm and a female egg, but it would not be alive and grow without divine assistance providing the spark of life. God is aware of all life because the Creator is the source of all life. Any power, ability, or talent that you have did not come about by solely your own doing. Even your mind and body was given to you so that you could choose your destiny. We may improve upon and expand our knowledge and human abilities in any area that we choose, but we couldn't do that without the foundation of life to build upon. We were created as infants so that we could evolve into our own destiny by our own free will.

I wouldn't want anyone else to have complete control over all Creation besides God. I cannot even begin to fathom the massive responsibility of establishing Divine Order for all life. Just one link out of balance in the ecosystem causes problems! I am grateful that God knows best and keeps that burden away from us and shields us from anything that is a feat that only God can do.

Duplicating reflections -
Photo by Sandy Briggs

Shine The Light

God wants to have a personal relationship with each and every person but does not force this upon us. When we evolve in good virtues, we reflect God's attributes more clearly through the mirror and become as one in spiritual likeness. *"may they all be one: as thou, Father, art in me, and I in thee, so also may they be in us, that the world may believe that thou didst send me. The glory that thou gavest me I have given to them, that they may be one, as we are one; I in them and thou in me, may they be perfectly one."*[32]

Falling farther from the light and into darkness

Photo by Sandy Briggs

Divinity is seen in us as long as we clearly reflect the divine essence of love and good will. When we don't reflect good will, then we fall away from the light and drift into darkness. When we digress away from the light, then God's invisible attributes become dimmer within us. The farther we stray from the light, the darker our character becomes and we fall into ruin.

The khristos reflects a bright light and clearly shines God's attributes. I saw in my vision that God foresaw that humankind would slip into darkness and this is why God sent the khristos spirit from above to bring the Word to humankind in the flesh. The state of khristos existed in the mind of God (in the spiritual realm) before the world was ever made. The things of the divine spirit eternally live in the realm of Light because this is where the spirit of God is revealed in the brightest clarity. The first image was sent to the realm of Earth as a testament to our highest potential, should we strive to evolve higher to emulate it.

On earth, Jesus became incarnate in the flesh through a woman for the purpose to bring enlightenment to humankind to conquer ignorance and to conquer mortality. God sent the renewing spirit, like a flame from fire, and sent it down into the domain of the earth's realm to give us light. This light came into the world by spiritual means, and was placed inside the womb of a woman (Mary) to become physically human, to give us a physical manifestation and an example of God's Word made manifest. The unblemished mirror image was placed inside the material dimension of a human being for us to follow by leading us closer to the light.

A word is first a thought before it is spoken just as God perceived a human likeness of the khristos before any action began on the phase of creating Man. God perceived a human likeness from the very beginning through God's invisible image. Jesus was born of flesh and ascended through all of the trials of life in the khristos state. Therefore, Jesus reflected God's invisible image, not by physical means, but by spiritual means. 2 Corinthians 4:4 says, *"the gospel of the glory of Christ, who is the very image of God, cannot dawn upon them and bring them light."* The truth is staring us in the face and people still have trouble understanding!

In my vision, I perceived of God providing various methods of safety nets to draw us back to the light before the Creation process began. God foresaw the evolution of all humanity before any action took place to create a world of material substance. Because God foresaw the problems of ignorance, God thought to send Jesus as *a human khristos* who would demonstrate a holy human for the very purpose to save humanity from the darkness (the state of not knowing). Jesus was one of many safety nets which was thought about beforehand. God also thought about angels and other spiritual entities to send when drastic measures were needed to guide humanity back on course. Life seemed to be like a strategy course of God's involvement only when it was absolutely necessary because it was important for humans to mature as much as possible by our own course in freedom. I can't stress enough how much God values our freedom and free will!

Jesus came to Earth from the spiritual realm to suffer at the hands of our ignorance to intercede for us because of our transgressions,[33] except many people rejected and crucified him just as they rejected the ways of God in ignorance. Spiritual truth was again too bright to see through opaqued eyes and yet the light is needed to dispel the darkness. The Word is the Living Truth from God, and the Truth became manifested in flesh. Everything that progressed in God's thought came to life! The Word was with God from the beginning.[34] Only the one who knows the truth from above can intercede to enlighten those who are veiled in ignorance. He (or she) who carries the divine truth comes to enlighten the world to combat ignorance, and in this way intercedes for our sins.

Christ as a man came to carry our sins upon himself[35] so that we may have access to God in the spirit while we were yet sinners (consumed by ignorance). He widened the door of communication for us so that we could have an easier opportunity to find a communion with God and to discover our own khristos reflection within. He came into this world to show us the way toward divinity. He also came to give us warning that those who will not choose to abandon their wrongdoing and won't turn back to the light will continue farther into darkness to the ruin of ourselves.

If we deliberately turn away from the light, then we are responsible for our own depravities and are held accountable for the misuse of our energy in this world. Jesus was sent by God to intercede to try to stop us from corrupting divine energy (sinning). He holds our iniquities to give us time to spiritually grow towards perfection through a continual renewing process of new beginnings (rebirth). When we reflect upon the truth and we begin to see beyond our ignorance, then our wrongdoing is chiseled away and our character becomes brighter. This is the whole point of our spiritual evolution. The secret that this world often hides is that we are able to emulate a Christ-like countenance within ourselves too! Then our sins will be completely forgiven and removed from us as well as from Christ's shoulders.

If we choose not to turn toward righteousness to have our sins cleared away by the appointed time, then our sins will remain upon ourselves as a laden soul on the Last Day of Judgment. As scripture points out: *"if we willfully persist in sin after receiving the knowledge of the truth, no sacrifice for sin remains."*[36] We cannot continue to remain in ignorance about this. Jesus is not guilty of our sins and he cannot be punished for eternity for our wrongdoing. (This is one of the reasons why Muhammad was given guidance to clear this up.) It is not fair for the innocent to be punished instead of the criminal. It is not just to punish the family, friends, or anyone else for the crimes someone else commits. God is just, therefore Jesus is exulted in Heaven. Jesus descended into the darkness of our world and bore the afflictions that people gave to him in this world in order to awaken our hearts to the ways of righteousness. He descended into this lower realm to wade through the ignorance of our world to shine the light of truth so that we may awaken and have access to a higher, better destiny.

Sin corrupts our character. It diminishes our khristos and sticks to us as dark weights. The more we corrupt our divine energy, the more weights of darkness attaches to our soul and pulls us downward and away from the heights of Heaven. If we are heavy with dark energy when we stand before God's presence, then God places our soul in a realm which befits it according to the intensity of our own weighted shackles. This is not done as a punishment. We are simply sieved and placed where we belong according to what we chose in our life as our destiny. A soul which likes and deliberately chooses the ways of darkness over light will not be at peace in the light because its essence rebels against perfection. Therefore, that soul doesn't belong in the light as long as that individual deliberately chooses to hold onto their shackles.

God doesn't force anyone to let go against their will. The only way to remove the heavy shackles is through our choice to take the shackles off. Shake off the lies we were taught by human leaders. We must choose to discard our own wicked ways and instead choose to emulate the essence of a higher state in order to be set free to learn about spiritual things through the Spirit. We must have an open heart and mind that will accept the spiritual teachings even when it may differ from what we were taught by humans. This is when the Holy Spirit will come upon you and cleanse you of impurities with the purifying fire. I testify to this because this happened to me in the year 2000. I was anointed with a spiritual flame just as it was experienced during Pentecost by the early Christians.

Unfortunately, our sins have become so heavy that we couldn't bear its weight without divine help. In ignorance, we didn't know what we were doing. Jesus, in the state of khristos consciousness, took pity on us with great compassion and took upon himself all of our iniquities to lighten our load. He knew that if we continued to rebel God and continued to choose the ways of darkness then our guilt remains.[37] Sin does not lead to eternal life in Heaven, therefore the unjust will never come into possession of the kingdom of God. If we knew better, would we still continue to choose the ways of darkness? Do we really want to destroy the whole human race? A warning still needed to be sent throughout the world so that we could make a more informed decision. For this reason is why God accepted my plea to help. We can no longer claim ignorance after we've received knowledge. The choice is yours alone to make.

For further clarity, a laden soul is one who carries his own burdens because he did not repent to embrace the ways of God to have his sins removed. Just because Jesus came to help set all people free from the bondage of sin, don't think that anyone is off scot-free from their sins if they do not repent. We can't continue to do destructive deeds of darkness. Our higher destiny is a lighter, brighter realm which lives in love, unity, harmony and peace. We may all ascend to that reflection by the renewing of our spirit with the divine spirit, which is the reason why God inspired men from all nations to deliver this message.

To arise to a more blissful, divine existence, each person must align their energy on the same side with divine attributes so that they may assimilate the same positive energy. In this way we also bring heaven on earth and our world may become more peaceful. Our society of crime and depravity may then evolve into a healed society with an upright character of morality and ethics.

Those who conform to the ways of God will have their dark energy (sins) placed on the scapegoat to be sent out away into the wilderness, far, far away to be remembered no more by God. God so loved the world that

He gave His beloved Son, (the first khristos image, that is without blemish) and whosoever believes in him, (for he told the truth, lived the truth, and was the truth), shall have everlasting life.[38] God is merciful, patient, and kind so we should not fear God when we stand face to face sincerely asking for forgiveness. God is the eternal source of love and life. This is why God provided a way for us to be reborn into the cycle of renewal on earth until we attain the state of khristos within.

Chapter Nine
Finding Unity with Divinity

After humans develop in knowledge and experience according to God's plan, each of the infinite sub-levels (generations of people) within the living mirror reflections could scale the heights toward perfection until they reach their highest potential. The final evolution of ourselves would remain as we fulfilled our own chosen destiny. No person would live eternally in the presence of God's fullness unless he or she freely chose to evolve to that level of existence. Jesus explained; *"everyone who commits sin is a slave. The slave has no permanent standing in the household, but the son belongs to it for ever."*[39]

Then I perceived that God may then choose to change the mirrors' angle of reflecting to move back to its prior position (for a lack of a better description, because God doesn't have any boundaries). This would bring an end to a polarized world and to a world of sin. Then we wouldn't have such trouble being tugged by negative energy which draws us away from God's realm of light. We would be more knowledgable about life after going through the human experience on a polarized planet.

This is how I perceive sin may one day be dissolved from our world. Sin did not exist in the beginning and as evident, it conflicts with divine attributes. God used sin temporarily to develop growth, knowledge and our individual character, all for the cause of giving freewill and eternal life to us. The mirrors were also used to reveal to ourselves who we are and where we belong. We developed according to our focus and use of energy.

Any person who deliberately chooses not to seek to evolve in the ways of righteousness will remain in a lower realm because they did not ascend toward the divine light in spirit. Therefore, they may be in danger of plummeting farther downward toward deeper darkness (ignorance) where there is no thinking, seeing, or doing in the deepest, lowest state. These people would be like dead stars because they do not shine (reflect light) of goodness. Their light is snuffed out and they become dormant, like death. This is how people are sorted, through our own choices, into those who choose life from those who choose to self destruct. It is within our realm on earth that life unfolds toward either destiny for each of us.

If we were to speculate as to whether the purest essence of man could turn into another God if they were to evolve as high as a human can go and perfectly reflect God's attributes in perfection, the answer is no. From what I understood through God's revelations, people can only reflect that *part* of God's essence that *they* are. A human may become a perfect human and in fact, this is God's will for each of us. We may evolve into a reflection of the original image, to emulate Christ, but we are not *another* God. Each of us remain a part of God that is always within the Source of Life. As long as a being is identified as an individual entity, then he or she is as a bubble floating in the sea of life. That's like comparing a drop of water with an ocean, or a bubble of air floating in the sky. The drop came from the ocean and may be a microcosm of the same essence, but the drop can either remain as an individual bubble or pop back to be "the all-in-all".

Even though this individual drop may be of the purest essence, it still does not equal the ocean from whence it came. This is what Jesus meant when he said that he and the Father were one (in spirit) and yet the Father is greater than he. During the formulation of early Christian doctrine, this was the issue that brought many bishops to fight over the relationship between Jesus the Christ and God The Father, (the teachings of

Arius versus Athanasius)! Religious leaders could find support for both views in scripture and a solid agreement could not be found. Because of the continual division between these views, the Roman Emperor Constantine in the year AD 325, decreed to suppress the teachings of Arius in support of the theology that Jesus was co-equal and co-eternal with God. The council then worked diligently to squash out any remaining disagreements but the teachings of Arius had already spread.

Constantine had good intensions to remove the heated controversy to try to force unity, but yet he had no right to control what they do not fully understand. If they did understand, then they wouldn't have debated for so long nor would they have forced others to conform to their specific view. We are supposed to use our minds and apply them with reason, but not to force others to conform against their will, especially when people don't know the truth from the spirit. Because of this forced theology, some people think that Christians believe in two gods, thus had fallen astray from monotheism, even though Christians *say* that they believe in one God. It looks like a contradiction to what they say from what they do.

Arius was a bishop (presbyter) who taught that Christ, the Son, was not consubstantial with God the Father. He taught that Jesus was not co-equal or co-eternal with God. We cannot contradict with the foundation of the Shema: *"Hear O Israel: The LORD our God, the LORD is one."*[40] This brings down the worship of polytheism and is why they taught that Jesus *is* God even though Jesus said nothing of the sort. Read further, and I will explain.

Replication reflections - Photo by Sandy Briggs

I can also understand why some people are lead to believe in more than one God. They see the many clear reflections of the One God emanated into separate reflections of entities which are perfected beings, thus perceiving them as multiple gods. Those beings who do reflect very high spiritual attributes are higher spiritual beings than those who do not reflect divine attributes. They are well advanced from the general population of humans. But those *entities* came from a greater Source.

While I was there in the heavenly realm during my near-death experience (NDE), there were others there with me, but I knew in my heart that they were not God. I was not God, although I merged back and forth with God's Consciousness through the Spirit. God is always supremely on top (greater) and all things are lesser (beneath), even if they clearly reflect divine attributes. God is in each of them and each of them are within the fullness of God. They can never escape beyond God's omnipresence. Each being is either aware or not aware of their connection to God, but we are all reflections of the One.

Actually I can see that both Arius' and Athanasian's views had some truth, but neither concept explains that only God is omnipotent (all powerful), omniscient (all-knowing) and omnipresent (always exists everywhere). Even though Jesus the Christ clearly reflected the true divinity of God in purity on earth, he could only access divine wisdom and knowledge through his communion with God. What prevents this *mirror replica* from being equal to God? The Bible explains: *"For the divine nature was his from the first; yet [Jesus] did not think to snatch at equality with God, but made himself nothing, assuming the nature of slave. Bearing human likeness, revealed in human shape, he humbles himself, and in obedience accepted even death"*[41]

If Jesus' mirror clearly reflects God's attributes, then Christ as a human identity would simply reflect a microcosm of God's attributes that were given to a human creature. He would not become a separate God. As scripture indicates: *"Before me there was no other god fashioned nor ever shall be after me."*[42]

Lucifer sought equality with God as another god. His proud, conceited, vain heart caused him to be cast out of Heaven because he steered people away from God to worship him in total adoration. Here is the difference. His very vain worship of himself was the imperfection which aborted him from the realm of light. We don't want to ascribe to Jesus of doing the same sin when he didn't even think to snatch at equality with God. Anyone who is working for God will point people toward God. They do not seek to be worshiped. Jesus said; *"Every kingdom divided against itself goes into ruin; and no town, no household that is divided against itself can stand."*[43]

God is eternal and this is why Jesus taught us to pray: "for **Thine** is the Kingdom and the power and the Glory for ever." All powers originate and flow forth from God. God's knowledge and understanding is unlimited, and God is everywhere at the same time. God may share any power and as much of it's likeness with whomever God chooses, but these powers still cannot manifest without God's approval and ultimate authority. Jesus explained: *"I do nothing on my own authority, but in all that I say, I have been taught by my Father."*[44] Jesus prayed to God the Father, he submitted to God, and he said that the Father was greater than he. Jesus thanked and consulted with God and taught us to pray to OUR FATHER. Jesus did not teach us to pray to himself. Jesus said; *"I do not care about my own glory."*[45]

Oh, boy! This has proved to be difficult for many Christians to believe, mainly because they were not permitted to understand this because of the dogma that they were forced to learn through church leaders. I was confused about this as well because Arius' and Athanasius' views could find support in scripture!

For this very reason is why many Jewish people won't embrace Jesus as a Messiah. They were taught that the Messiah is not God but was sent by God. We are not to worship anything or anyone in God's stead. This is also why the Archangel Gabriel came to the prophet Muhammad to clarify this misunderstanding to humankind. It was not to punish people for not believing in Muhammad! This misunderstanding about Christ is why the Jews, Christians and Muslims continue to violently disagree. Who is brave enough to rise above their errant teachings? All of them have many misunderstandings among their beliefs, which were forced upon us. This is why our world continues to suffer with conflict and war.

We must apply our minds to understand through divine eyes so that we may emulate righteousness like Christ. This is our destiny. *"For my children you are, and I am in travail with you over again until you take the shape of Christ."*[46] Christ does what he sees the Father do. We too must follow the example of Christ and seek to reflect God's goodness. We must continue to grow into higher dimensions and seek deeper knowledge of the divine nature.

God is the true eternal Source of all life, therefore there are not now, nor will there ever be any other source who presides above all things. The Source remains the source. The reflection of a flame within the mirror cannot provide light without its source. If the original flame is removed, then its reflection is removed as well. God always exists and emanates the divine essence, and is seen in those who reflect divine attributes, such is the nature of the spirit.[47] This is why righteousness is eternal and sin leads to destruction. The continual destruction from our wrongdoing is a result of our forced misunderstandings. We don't want sin to be eternal and neither does God. God wanted to be as a Father among His children. The children did not exist before their father. *"For God knew his own before ever they were, and also ordained that they should be shaped to the likeness of his Son, that he might be the eldest among a large family of brothers."*[48] *"I will be a father to you, and you shall be my sons and daughters."*[49]

This is what I witnessed in Heaven! The glory of God that I saw in Heaven was not Jesus, although Jesus was and is very, very high in authority. Jesus is like the first image of the candle in the mirror, the brightest reflection of God's invisible attributes in purity, except in human form. Jesus was the first that descended into the earth realm and ascended back to God, the first to return from the dead.[50] If anyone would want to argue with this point, then I will say to them that the Word is the Truth, and scripture explains that Jesus is our brother.[51] God told me in a vision/ memory that there is no other original Source and we need not speculate further into anything that is false. I felt resolute that to speculate further would just be going around in circles, eventually leading me to the same conclusion.

"And may God, the source of all fortitude and all encouragement, grant that you may agree with one another after the manner of Christ Jesus,

so that with one mind and one voice you may praise the God and Father of our Lord Jesus Christ."[52]

I saw in my vision about Creation that the whole purpose of Creation is because God wanted to share love with us. The feminine hemisphere of the eternal Consciousness wanted to pour out Her love and share all that God is. God doesn't need anything or anyone for sustenance, but the tremendous love of God could not be contained without sharing. Love had to burst forth, and so God wanted interaction with life and likewise, wanted the khristos *living image* to have interaction with companions as well. God fully understood that it was not good for man to be alone. It is so awesome what I was shown in a vision about this! How can anyone call this merely a dream? How long would a dream be to contain all of the information that I have shared so far, and yet this is just a pinch of the cupful that I was given! I am always in awe of the things I learn through visions and revelations. I pray that this information will help to make a difference in our world for the better!

I then thought to myself; if all people knew everything and there wasn't anything else to know, wouldn't we become bored with ourself and of life? I reasoned that it is fulfilling to have infinite spiritual growth and expanding knowledge in all things. This makes life interesting as we discover everything. That's also why God didn't want to be alone and wanted fellowship with life. This makes perfect sense to me! That's the purpose of Creation.

Creation began with the desire of love. The world was created because of love and for love. The abundant love that God contains had to be shared and burst forth like an explosion of energy! The very fact that we exist is proof of God's love for us. Pure divine love is stronger, richer, and fuller than any love that we know here on earth. Once I felt the pureness of God's everlasting love, it was clear to me that the love on this earth is distorted and tainted. I long for the *living fountain* of love which is eternal. We were created from God's love and we were taught that the greatest of all is love. God's first commandment is to love God with all of our heart, mind, and soul and to seek God with all of our strength. The second commandment is like it in that we are to love one another. Love is the foundation of life.

Chapter Ten

The Bridge

Our world has many mysteries to solve and if we wish to seek the truth, then we need to be free to search in freedom without hindrance or thought control. We may stumble along the way, but at least it also opens doors to learn. The alternative is never knowing what is yet to be discovered and not having the opportunity to find out. The truth is 'what is' without deception. People may prove truths through discovered facts but we also need to keep an open mind toward possibilities for further disclosure.

I chose to explore the unknown by keeping my heart open to spirituality, seeking testimonies and learning from personal experiences. These discoveries that I found may unlock some of the secrets of life that this world so desperately needs. It may help bring humanity closer together through understanding. Peace in our world could be possible if all people would join together on the bridge of unity. This bridge connects all varieties of people as one great humanity. It allows our unique differences to co-exist together just as a field of all kinds of flowers co-exist in the same field or garden. Our field is the planet. My goal is one with God's goal to see a world living in harmony instead of dividing ourselves in war over our differences.

I have found that there are many similar explanations about the information that I received from my visions and revelations that are written in scriptures among various religions. Therefore, I recognize a core foundation which unifies all religions. I hope to open up and invite more people to find a more in-depth understanding of these similarities within the religious mysteries and show a connection that will help bring all of us together. Harmony yields peace, therefore, we must come together to find a oneness of all humanity.

I cannot deny what has happened in my life and my experiences of unusual phenomena have opened my mind to things I would not have known otherwise. Even with all that I have discovered, I wish to find even a deeper understanding of how and why these mysteries occur. There is always more to learn. It is not easy to describe or relate to others who had not experienced such spiritual things in clear, conceivable words. Some things that I testify to are so extraordinary that I do not understand them yet. But yes, they are quite real.

To me, the solid truth of reality is only what I had personally experienced. When a person shares their testimonies, other people have not touched it personally, therefore, we can only choose to believe them or not. This is also where faith develops. It is called faith because we had not touched or known it personally. After we personally experience something, then it goes beyond faith and becomes *known* because it becomes actualized in our life.

People associate faith with religion because they trust that the scriptures they study were given by intervention of a higher deity, our Source, our Creator. But faith is bigger than religion. Faith does not necessarily have to be connected to religion, (especially if that religion is corrupt), and yet faith is connected to our Creator because our world is what our Creator created. Religion is just the guidance that was meant to bind us together, but something went wrong.

Faith and truth reaches beyond religion and encompasses our whole world, our whole existence, our whole galaxy; all that there is. Many things are unseen, untouchable, unrealized, and yet they exist. We can't see the air, but we breathe it and feel it as a wind. We can't see or touch a flavor, but we can differentiate between a crisp juicy apple and an onion as we taste it. There are different ways to discover things, but not always with our physical senses. Consider emotions. We can't physically touch emotions, yet we feel them as moods. A person may feel various states of moods while not talking or moving, but the intensity of emotion is the seed which sprouts some type of thought or action. Through observation of a creature's action, the emotion is revealed. Because we have a world with both visible and invisible things, many people have difficulty in believing in a Creator because they have not seen nor heard God. They have difficulty believing and having faith in the unseen deity because they want evidence and physical proof that they can tangibly touch, see, hear, taste or smell. But there is more to life than the physical reality.

    I cannot ever be a nonbeliever of God because I have gone past faith and became a witness of the reality of our Creator beyond our physical realm. I had to go through a spiritual veil to actually find our spiritual home. I can no longer doubt the existence of other realms and our Creator because I personally experienced these. Some realms are seen and others are unseen. I experienced both. This does not mean that I understand everything in totality of what I experienced, but I can share what I observed in the spirit and what I do understand to bear witness.

    I experienced proof of God and I see proof of God in all of creation. I understand why some people have difficulty in believing in God's reality and I do not seek to criticize anyone for their unbelief. People were given free will and I respect people's freedom of choice. It is difficult for many to embrace things without first-hand proof, therefore many people simply remain skeptical and wait to witness. Blessed are those who do not need to have proof and still believe.

I had a near-death/out-of-body experience more than thirty years ago and it is still an awesome experience to me. I did not realize that I was outside of my physical body until I returned back into my physical body. I had no idea that was possible until it just spontaneously happened! When I contemplate about this, I am still in awe about this miraculous wonder. I don't know how I got there or where 'there' is, or how to go back 'there'. But, I was there, in Heaven, in another dimension of heightened existence. It was more real than my life on earth. I was taken to a place of pure bliss and pure light. The light was brighter than a snow-and-ice covered field with the sun shining on it, except the brightness did not hurt my eyes.

In our realm, we cannot look at the sun or we would burn our retina, feel excruciating pain and blind ourselves. The light that I was in and experienced felt very calm, tranquil, peaceful, and loving. It was also very exhilarating and rejuvenating. I saw with exact precision and crisp detail that my vision in this realm doesn't have. Everything that I saw during my spiritual experience was in clear, perfect focus. I had a sight beyond human ability. While I was able to view in this ultra sense of visual sight, I could also view from different angles or distances at the same time. I have no idea how I was able to do that! I never even thought about that possibility because we cannot do this on earth.

In the same way, my hearing and emotions were also enhanced to a greater degree in Heaven. I did not hear with my ears, but sound was like the wind that flowed through me. I didn't need physical ears. I could feel emotions from the sounds, from the light, and from the presence of others without looking at them. My sense of knowing was enhanced and I knew that Who I saw was/is God the Father. God may and does manifest to us in the spiritual realm and there was a constant presence of love and safety that saturated my being in Heaven.

When I saw God, I instantly knew that this is the Creator of all life.

The Bridge

No one had to tell me who this was because I felt it, I knew it. I identified God as masculine because that was how I perceived Him during this particular event. This was as much God to me as I also experienced fifteen years later as an unseen *presence* in other experiences, such as I shared in chapter four which revealed the contents of this book to me. God held within him both masculine and femine hemispheres and sometimes I could not detect any gender. I am still open to the possibility that another witness may perceive our Creator as something different from my experiences. After all, I'm not the one who is in charge of what God chooses to do. Even though I saw with my spiritual eyes how God chose to reveal Himself to me in the spirit, I know that I must keep the door open for further revelation. In the earth's realm, people fight over these discrepancies instead of tolerating other perceptions of interrelated truth. It's important not to focus only on one small portion of a puzzle without seeing the whole picture. With things in the spirit, we must keep an open mind to embrace anything that will be revealed in the spiritual realms.

Consider this scenario that a friend once told me. Two people are walking side by side along the coastline. As they talked to one another, one is facing the sand dunes while the other is facing the ocean waves. If they didn't observe the whole scenery around them, they saw and described two completely different scenes. Both of them were correct and sharing the truth. So if I use the pronoun of "he", it's because I experienced God as the Father, and yet I know from other experiences that God is also the Mother.

I testify that God was filled with a magnitude of pure powerful love that this world does not fathom. He was perfect and yet how do I describe what is perfect when I am not perfect and have not known total perfection within myself? He was simply beyond me and beyond any human being. He will always be very difficult to describe.

God radiated a glorious, perfect love and there was no chance of there ever being anything that wasn't perfection and love within His presence of 'being'. From what I saw and felt, God would not wish harm to anyone. I can't even fathom God being wrathful or jealous as it describes Him in the Old Testament! These qualities are the antitheses of the One I witnessed in Heaven. Yet His presence was commanding with utmost respect and authority. My life was completely in His hands.

Although accepting divine guidance is the epitome of faith, not all religious guidance is understood and practiced without deception or distortion. If a teaching cannot possibly lead the world toward peace without infringing on the rights of the people then their perception is flawed. Religion is helpful but only when it is understood through the spirit of divine truth. Divine guidance is infallible when it is understood as God intends. When we learn through the spirit, the communication comes with a *knowing* through a direct connection of emotions and visions. In this way many of the teachings that had lead people to hate and to kill one another can clearly be seen as defective teachings.

Divine guidance is the foundation that all prophets and messengers have received from the same spiritual Source. But here is where the difficulty of human comprehension comes into play when they try to share it. Because each person has their own point of view, their own understanding, each of us may have variable ideas of what we're taught when we hadn't experienced God's Spirit firsthand. Even though the ultimate Truth is unchanging, people's perceptions are variable and not clear. I have seen how words are misunderstood and taken out of context. I can see the difficulty that past prophets and messengers of God have had in trying to explain esoteric knowledge into words which are inadequate for describing things not experienced by others. How does one teach the carnal mind the things of the divine nature when they don't understand it and without having accurate words to explain? I'm trying my best but I hope and pray that the words and the presentation that I chose to explain will be understood with clarity.

I know that God always honors our free will. I could even choose not to share what was divinely revealed to me, but because I saw and understood it as much as I did, I also realize that it would be a very wrong decision not to share it. I was shown too much and I know that if I found a way to get the message out then it must be able to help humanity. Why else would the Holy Spirit send me so much divine insight that's beyond what I would ever need just for my personal life? Why should only I be privy to it when it could help all people?

It was also revealed to me that God foresaw the dilemma of where our free will would lead many of us into a vile and vicious lifestyle on earth. This is why it was necessary to intervene now and again. God made plans to retrieve us even before we ever came to live on earth. The extreme suffering that humans inflict upon others would make it necessary for God to intervene and impose His authority and to establish rules of conduct. These rules were brought about because we harm one another, otherwise we would be left to our own will without the need for intercession of divine guidance.

God made an everlasting promise with Noah that never again would the entire earth be flooded to destroy all creatures. The covenant with God is that all humans should live an upright life to receive blessings from God throughout our lives. We would be cursed when we'd turn to evil ways. That's the consequence of our choices. Good behavior begets blessings and harmful behavior begets detrimental things.

Unfortunately, religion became so complicated as men tried to control and dominate it with their own viewpoints before they became a genuine witness to its spiritual truth. In this way, men took away freedom from religion and it became an institution of coercion and persecution.

They even tried to silence the feminine voice and used her as a scapegoat for their chauvinistic perception.

This turned religion into an oppressive system which removed our freedom to pursue our destiny. When our individual human perspective of religion doesn't match divine Truth, then religion becomes an apostasy and leads people astray from discovering God. Those who follow the spirit will discover God because God is only found in spirit of truth. I did not understand what that meant until I found God in spirit and in truth. As a female, I was embraced and accepted by God.

I wonder about the alternative. Would life be worth living if we were told exactly what to do from God in every situation? This would prevent anyone from making harmful choices. What would our life entail if we did not have free will to make our own decisions? We wouldn't have our individual freedom if we weren't allowed to make harmful choices. Why weren't humans created with perfect attitudes so that we wouldn't fall astray? Could humans live without freedom? I suppose we could, but then we would be like robots, all thinking and reacting alike. But as history reveals over and over again, people struggle without their freedom and they are driven to break free. How could robots be pleasing to a loving and compassionate God unless he were only a self-centered megalomaniac who wanted to be served by slaves? Why would God ever need to be served by slaves when God is self-sufficient? Our individuality proves that God is not self serving.

Why then, did God create humans in diversity? We wouldn't be human without individuality through our diverse appearances, diverse voices, diverse intellect, talents and skills, etc. How could we learn without the freedom to think, to question and explore? Would we want to live without this freedom? But that's what makes our life interesting! I don't think that I would want to be a mindless robot.

The Bridge

What did God see in humankind that made free will the better alternative, even per chance we might fall astray, than giving absolute dictation to follow without freedom? That lifestyle reminds me of how dictators rule with fascism. A totalitarian government is against freedom and doesn't allow for free will of the people. They rule for their own selfish aggrandizement without concern, compassion or love for those who serve them. A dictator is feared and his people are oppressed. What makes any human dictator more valuable than the lives of all the people he enslaves? Because he says so? This makes no sense to me and I would never freely choose to live like that, especially since I know what it's like to have my freedom.

I can't stand being coerced, especially when it is very likely that the person in authority could be a ruthless, self-centered megalomaniac. I can see how some arrogant, power-hungry people would want complete control over others, but it can't be in the best interest of all people under him if they were not permitted to question him if he was corrupt. Why would anyone want to serve a ruler who cares nothing about their safety and welfare? It can't be fair to force people against their will to submit to an authority figure who cares nothing for his people and reins with torture and corruption. Why should a brutal, immoral human be served as a superior authority and ruler when his actions are full of corrupt, vile crimes against his people? Surely this is not pleasing to God since our whole world was created to honor our free will. The people have a right to rise up against the deplorable violence used against them.

The God that I found was not like an authoritarian dictator at all! But isn't it bizarre that so many religious despots teach that God is like this and so they base the foundation of their faith on fear instead of love. They pound on about God's wrath and eternal punishment with fire and brimstone and other guilt-ridden lectures! Their aggressive warning instills so much fear that people feel forced to obey these religious dictators, and recede from questioning their absolute authority to seek real answers. But fear is not of God. This is so contradictory to what I witnessed in the heavenly realm! Yes, God is above all and has complete power over all things, but not as an egotistical, self-serving authoritarian. God always has ultimate authority, yet doesn't abuse us by forcing us to do things against our will. There can be no absolute control over people if we were given free will and as was revealed to me, God did not want to take away our free will. This is one of the reasons why God stays hidden to this realm, to permit us freedom of our choices, even about believing in God!

God certainly is not *forcing* people to believe or to conform to anything, otherwise God, being all-powerful, would be dictating absolute authority each moment of our life. God doesn't need human armies to conquer His own Creation. The Creator can create anything that He wills, and indeed has, so why would an all-knowing, all-powerful God create humans to go to battle against each other after choosing to create us in diversity? Our loving Creator is not playing any cruel games with us!

I clearly see that a life without freedom of choice would be a life of suppression and oppression under an absolute authoritarian dictator. If God wanted absolute obedience from us, then why are sinners permitted to make mistakes? If we were not permitted to make mistakes, then why aren't more people dropping dead each time we make them? That way of rule is the complete opposite and illogical from what was revealed to me about how and why our world was created. People weren't created as clones with identical thought patterns. We were created with an abundance of varying talents, interests and personalities. This variety of diversity is reflected in all creation and it gives life beauty and fascinating experiences.

A perfect Creator is fair, loving and merciful to all. God values us for who we are and permits us the freedom to pursue our destiny according to the level of our ability and at our own pace of comprehension. Perfect love does not dictate authority or instill fear. Perfect love banishes fear![53] Constant fear only produces resentment and revolt. Perfect love respects the rights of another person's will while teaching with care, compassion, understanding and tolerance. Isn't it logical that an all-knowing God would be tolerant and understanding of our weaknesses and mistakes? Wouldn't God understand why each of us does as we do?

I now understand that many people would have a very difficult time accepting direct divine revelations from God if their heart and mind were not able to accept what they would be shown. Many people would reject it when it did not parallel their exact religious beliefs. So many people were brainwashed into thinking that God wanted us to go to war to force people into submission and to hate those who differ. How will these people ever see the beauty of diversity? Isn't it evident in itself that God chose diversity for the human race over unthinking, unfeeling robots?

Some of the things that I was shown were difficult for me to swallow, all-the-while I knew them to be the truth. They were difficult because they conflicted with ideas that I was taught in this world. I had to re-examine the scriptures from a heightened all-embracing viewpoint in order to understand it through a universal perception. The truth is so logical and yet it is so difficult for humans to grasp. It's so bizarre to explain this. Who would think that the truth would be so difficult to share? Especially when there are so many people who want to know the truth.

All of us are caught between the discrepancies of the ways of our world and its twisted ideologies of dogma. This made it difficult to embrace the correct point of view that was revealed through divine intercession. It is difficult to keep our mind and heart free of judgment when we become so set in our ways with what we were taught from human authorities. We gave our trust to them. Some things that they taught were correct yet some things were not.

It was difficult for me at first to accept that so much of what religious authorities teach are nothing but defective human opinions and are not absolute truths at all. I respected their authority as a child, but I did not find God by following all of their teachings. I discovered God by not rejecting what the spirit revealed to me. Yet these human despots demand the epitome of authority so much that they threaten those who oppose them with horrible consequences and anathema. Their fear indoctrinated religious teachings stifle seekers from searching in truth. That's why so many of God's prophets, messengers and servants were martyred! The religious despots have slammed the door in men's faces so that few dare to confront them!

Since I was shown these divine visions, I see how very wrong it is to permit any human to impose absolute guidelines of authority without permitting people to seek answers and to investigate their teachings with our sense of reason and logic with our conscience. It's difficult to break away from the lies we had been fed with so much guilt and fear. Luckily, the spirit sets us free.

Absolute authority by any human is sure to have flaws in some form or another for no person is perfect, (except perhaps those who clearly reflect God's unblemished image). We may know only what God discloses to us. No human is all knowing! No human knows all of the answers, and all of the religious authorities do not have the exact same view about religion and life. Each of us must discover divine truth through our own efforts by finding our connection back to the true Source. Each of us must use our freedom to explore beyond stagnant ideology which can never lead us to God. God is to be found by a seeker of truth and I testify that this can be done through the spirit.

Chapter Eleven

A God of Wrath and Vengeance?

My Thoughts

In the light of truth, I contemplated further. Perhaps if God saw the *need* to show wrath, then it may be done in necessity to save our world from extinction. There has to be a good reason for everything God does. And so I dabbled with reason even what's revealed from above because I know that the higher truth of all things is forever deeper and unfathomable to any person. I realized that God protects and sustains us because we are loved. If God did not love us, then we simply would not exist. This is why I can't fathom God doing anything that wasn't overall for our own good. So I wonder, is the description of God's character accurate in the Old Testament? Maybe the words "wrath", "jealous" and "vengeance" were the reflection of what people perceived of God at that time but wasn't completely understood. So many people reject the Old Testament description of God because it portrays an unfair and cruel deity. How could God be unfair and cruel if God is just and perfect love? These qualities are in conflict and does not fit in with perfection as I was shown and taught through the spirit. Therefore, God's actions as recorded in the Old Testament may have been misunderstood. Is religion practiced without any deception? Obviously not. I understood through the spirit that any branch of religion was half true and half misunderstood.

Perhaps if God's authoritative character was not shown in this powerful way, then the human race would have continued to follow the path of destruction and then would eventually become extinct. Some things seem to be vengeful from our perspective when actually may be done for our own benefit for the future. For example, children do not like receiving consequences for being naughty, and they think that their parents are cruel and bossy when they do. They don't perceive their parents' actions as coming from love and concern for their own safety and benefit. They later discover that they learned to be more responsible and not to repeat their mistakes because of the authority and discipline of our elders who have had prior experiences and wisdom. (I'm not talking about abusive discipline.) In other words, we learned from our mistakes.

It's your choice. Do you choose to believe that God created people to throw them into hell to suffer for eternity? Or do you believe that God created people in diversity to experience life in diverse ways and to learn from life through our own choices? Do you choose to believe that God is loving, compassionate and merciful or do you choose to believe that God is hateful, wrathful and full of vengeance?

If people can understand and embrace that there is an afterlife, then they should also understand that our soul does not die. Even as tragic as war and death is in our world, the part of us that animates our body, our soul, lives on. Death is only a temporary state, an illusion of life to allow a period for transformation to prepare for rebirth. It was revealed to me that the afterlife attracts like or relative qualities unto itself. The closer we are in likeness as we evolve toward God's attributes, then the closer our being is conformed toward goodness and our rebirth will reflect the same. If the souls of most people on earth obtain this heightened goodness, then our world would also transform into a deeper, fuller state of goodness. Our world is what we collectively make it.

A God of Wrath and Vengeance...My Thoughts

I sincerely believe that the reason that God chose to inspire certain individuals was to help guide the rest of humankind without *forcing* them to understand, where they may use their *own* sense of reasoning and free will. Surely God has the power to force people to follow divine guidance, but doesn't because God respects our free will. We have to make our own choices and then take responsibility for those choices. Although, on the downside of free will, people do make harmful choices. This is the dilemma of free will.

God was so tolerant of our free will that (for example, in the days of Noah), people were permitted to plummet far down and away from the light until it was inevitable that humans would corrupt and annihilate our whole human race if we didn't change the condition of our heart. The wickedness upon the earth was so great that if we continued any further as we were headed, all humans would have continually suffered agony from our own actions of destruction. We would have made life on earth a living hell for all of us. This is what made it necessary for God to intervene with our lives. It was necessary for God to interject guidance and to inspire people of God's choosing so that they would help influence others on the right path, and yet continue to permit free will to remain. Those with whom God chooses to receive divine guidance are only to give warning and share what we were given so that others may contemplate and explore what we share. We are not to force others into submission, although it would benefit the survival of the human race if all people would heed the message. It is still the responsibility of each person to choose what they accept. Any other way of coercion against the will of the people becomes oppression.

A friend of mine who also has prebirth memories was told that this was the spiritual battle which caused the angels so much trouble in the heavens that there had to be a separation and a choice. One view wanted to force people to obey without free will (the way of strict laws with no room for error) so that we would be forced to conform without revolt. The other view wanted to permit people to learn from life through the consequences of their choices. (This way allowed people to make mistakes but to reprieve any negative consequences through learned lessons. The outcome of life would reflect their choices.) Earth would be the place to observe which way was more productive.

The first example removed our freedom, hopefully so we wouldn't attempt to do wrongs. Even though the punishments were severe, people could not keep the strict laws. God had already planned for humans to strive for freedom because freedom is an essence of divinity. The polarity was to be imprisoned. The way of strict laws lead to punishment and death. It bound us to be enslaved by our crimes.

I've seen through the error of human religious authorities who dictate their own point of view as absolute even though they hadn't received the Holy Spirit to guide them. They think that their human interpretations are Divine and so coerce all people to submit to them. I realize that it wasn't the complete fault of these authorities if they were manipulated and controlled by previous human authorities who imposed absolute authority of obedience to follow certain rules of conduct. They dictated specific traditions, customs and ideology of their own making and then said that it couldn't be questioned. This flawed hierarchy of human authority is corrupted by power at many levels. The leaders whom we've trusted thought that they were teaching what was correct. They insisted that it was unthinkable to question human authorities because they were "schooled" as the experts. If humans were infallible there wouldn't be such corruption in our world, but unfortunately, the nature of all people are capable of error.

So often, people with corrupt motives step into the seat of authority (whether religious, governmental or social system). They don't live righteously nor do they align themselves towards good virtues which would enable them to rule correctly with dignity and fairness. Instead, these corrupt leaders seek power for themselves and rebel righteousness by refusing to repent of their faults. They choose instead to conceal and to repeat their crimes instead of acknowledging and repenting their wrong behavior. When religious authorities can not be questioned or can not be held accountable for their wrongdoing, they become conceited, vain, and full of self pride. Vain, arrogant leaders think that they are above the law and they don't abide by the laws they preach, thereby become hypocrites. When they break their own laws, they don't consider giving up their position of authority for the good of the people. Leaders who value their own absolute power and prestige higher than the rights of others are blind guides. They fall astray as they lust for ultimate power and glory and expect to be worshiped by people. People who fall astray commit harmful deeds and despise the truth. They avoid the light because their deeds are dark.

"Here lies the test: the light has come into the world, but men preferred darkness to light because their deeds were evil. Bad men all hate the light and avoid it, for fear their practices should be shown up. The honest man comes to the light so that it may be clearly seen that God is in all he does." [54]

There upon, megalomaniacs migrate toward the opposite inclination of goodness because they focus on their own self interest of individual superiority rather than the all-embracing view of harmony and respect for all people. Too much arrogance and vain desires in power corrupt people. This is what many people do not grasp. No one has the right to force their point of views and then force others to submit without giving people the opportunity to choose, otherwise this path will lead them into a lifestyle full of wickedness again! It leads to constant bloodshed and a life without love and security.

God created in diversity so that we could be uniquely whomever we wanted to be in freedom, although He hoped that we would *choose* to follow the path of goodness along the way. Unfortunately with freedom of will, there was always that vice which permits us to decide our path between what is good or bad - healthy or harmful. As I observed the vision of human spiritual evolution, I saw that people migrated toward likenesses of themselves because they conflicted with their opposition and they searched for harmony with their own identity. Those who migrated toward God's attributes were lead by unconditional love and philanthropic views, while those who migrated away were lead down the path of harming others, which ultimately harmed themselves.

Those who oppose all of the ways of righteousness are apostates of God when all of their attributes reflect corruption. They stray farther and farther away from righteousness until they ultimately live only for themselves (egotists), with absolutely no concern for others. They become intolerant and haters of anything dissimilar or different from them and have no conscience of the harm they inflict onto others. They even feel that they have a right to destroy any and all opposition and competition!

Murder is the utmost example of intolerant action to destroy its adversary without justification - simply because it is different or disliked. They have no respect for diversity. (Self defense is another topic.) An egotist's focus becomes self-centered and they don't have any guilt about stealing what does not belong to them because they are driven only by what *they* want for their own personal gain. Their emotions of love become tainted with greed and hedonism. Other people serve no purpose other than to satisfy their own self interest. When a person like this sits in the seat of authority, then that society becomes corrupt. For this reason is why scripture guides us not to worship any human.

God is perfection, truth, goodness, love, etc., and the opposite is corruption, deceit, evil, hate, etc. Humankind's actions fall somewhere in-between perfection and corruption. Each person is responsible to learn the delicate balance to use our own free will without crossing over the line to infringe on the rights of others or to intentionally bring them harm. Each person has the freedom to choose the way which guides their life.

As more and more people were inclined towards corruption, there evolved the need to give guidance to humankind to try to guide us back to the path of goodness; as a shepherd draws his stray sheep with his staff. This is why Moses received the 'Words of the Covenant' (The Ten Commandments) which directs humankind not to steal, lie, cheat, murder, covet what is not ours, etc. Then humankind was left to use this information along with our reasoning skills and conscience to help guide us on to a better path.

After the Covenant was given, ancient rabbis and lawmakers drew up 613 laws from the covenant. Their "follow to the letter" laws required us to be justified by what we *do in accordance to those laws*, but no one could live perfectly without breaking such concrete laws because it was against our nature of free will. The laws became black or white and very strict so that the people were oppressed with punishments without mercy, justice or good faith.[55] No one could be perfect according to their laws which they taught as doctrines, but were actually the commandments of men.[56] The free will of the people to make their own choices were violated thus their laws bound us to sin. *"It is evident that no one is ever justified before God in terms of law.[57]"*

Humankind evolved in this way until it became necessary for God to send other messengers, prophets, and teachers to explain the intricacies of the law in which lawmakers nullified God's guidance. Humankind was permitted to continue in their ways until God saw it necessary to send a *living* example of His guidance. Jesus was sent as the *living* Word to explain and show to the people by example to clarify where they went wrong. He was not sent to condemn people for their crimes, but to guide humankind back toward righteousness, back toward the proper covenant. Jesus showed the correct use of mercy, tolerance, forbearance, forgiveness, and sacrifice which broke the bonds of the written law. This gave humankind freedom from the chains which bound us to the law of sin. This opened the door to bring the salvation of humankind to find eternal life in a higher state of existence.

As people multiplied and migrated to different parts of the globe, we each needed someone within our own community to guide us. Thereupon God chose individuals from among the many communities to receive divine guidance in accordance with each unique clan of people and according to *their* needs. Therefore, each nation was guided by God's chosen messengers. Unfortunately, many people (not all) chose to become prejudiced and bigoted against anything that wasn't of their own clan's unique understanding when we eventually migrated back together during trade and habitat changes. It was God's wish that we should learn from each other through our diversities so that we would grow emotionally, intellectually and spiritually sound.

The life of righteousness must be tolerant of our diversity. Some people chose to learn to live in harmony with other clans in patience and tolerance. It is possible. Yet others wanted to take control to dominate above the other diverse clans because they felt superior to them. Then came the need for the oppressed clans to defend themselves from their oppressors, thus evolved the atrocities of war. Our unique customs had intertwined and evolved with both good and bad practices from each side; some by force of tyrants, others through our choice.

To this day, each individual person is caught between the choice to follow the path to live upright lives or to suffer consequences when we make harmful decisions. Each of us has an inner gauge which guides our conscience so that we may use our own sense of reason. Unfortunately some of us don't seek to follow an upright life even though we know deep inside the difference between right and wrong. Because some of us are lead with prejudiced and bigoted views, our world reaped the consequences. We evolved with fighting over which human authority gains the power to rule over others in superiority.

Megalomaniacs who sit in the seat of absolute power won't embrace the harmony of the ways of peace and their leadership will become tyrannical. This is why it is detrimental to any society to place any corrupt man in the seat of absolute power to dictate complete control and absolute submission to his supremacy. It is to the detriment of humanity when we choose to fight against people of differing backgrounds simply because they differ in culture and ethnicity. Surely to reject toleration of our diversities is the result of refusing to question and face our own culture's faults and to relinquish our own illusion of superiority. No one is seeking peace while they seek to annihilate free will in others.

This reminds me of the lessons in the scriptures about Lucifer. His iniquity was vain glory and he sought equality with our Creator who alone is perfection. His proud, conceited, vain heart was the cause of him being cast out from Heaven because he wanted to steer people away from God to worship him in total adoration. Anyone who is working for God does not wish to steer anyone away from God and they do not seek to be worshipped. Instead, they guide people to the ways of the divine and point people toward God for the good of all people.

Time and time again, we see uprisings of clans of people who believe that they are superior to others. They seek to divide themselves from the mainstream population because they don't want to assimilate with others. They are motivated to condemn others, when their own clan is no better. Would we be created in diversity simply to hate diversity? That makes no logical sense to me. It's when people are blinded by prejudice that they can't rightly distinguish between friends or foes. Since prejudiced people can't see into another person's heart, it's easier for many of them to choose sides based upon worldly thinking and prejudices which are viewed as differences. Therefore, instead of humanity seeking spiritual likenesses of universal virtues (kindness, honesty, respect, etc.), many of us regressed and migrated towards physical likenesses that we could see and identify within ethnic and cultural commonalities. This behavior developed problems with social issues because they forfeited the path of tolerance in exchange for feeling superior, leading them on the path to divide and conquer.

    We can't make allowances and excuses for faults and hate crimes that were committed by our own *people* while condemning others for the same crimes. This behavior develops hypocrisy. People fall astray when we permit hatred from prejudice to grow until we act out our aggressions with deeds of iniquities against the rights of others. We have become hypocrites when we commit crimes that we condemn in others, while doing nothing to correct ourselves. A just person should not do what they deem to be wrong behavior in others. This understanding has always been desperately lacking in human society, and it follows the golden rule which most religions teach; "Do unto others as you would have them do unto you". Therefore, we certainly did reap what we sowed in corruption!

    I had seen in a vision that God always watches over our choices and takes whatever means is necessary to assist us while trying not to use force until it is absolutely necessary. God acts through necessary increments and variations of intervention to guide us back on track. It isn't until the human race generally reaches the stage which becomes indolent of following the path of righteousness and floundering on destruction that God erupts with the strongest of intervention. His intervention in our lives was only to guide us back toward the path of righteousness so that the human race could survive, and then we were left to our own freedom of choice again to test our understanding. I saw that God always has a plan to counteract our own choices of mistakes when we go too far down the wrong path. I understood that the last resort was to force us to follow righteousness, but if need be to save humankind, God was prepared to use force as a *temporary* guide until we knew better.

This makes sense to me when scripture explains how we were close prisoners in the custody of the law and that the law was a temporary measure that was given as a tutor to conduct us until faith came by following the gospel message that Jesus Christ revealed so that we might receive the promised Spirit through faith.[58] His hope for humankind was that we would not need to be lead with force but rather we would learn from our mistakes before it got to that point of damage. It was our responsibility to learn from life; to compare the consequences of following the ways of sin as opposed to following the ways of an upright life.

This makes me wonder if this is why the Old Testament describes God as an overseer of force. It is written in the book of Genesis 6:5, in the time of Noah, that God was sorry that He had made people on earth because we had done much evil and that human thoughts and inclinations were *always* evil. It sounds as though humanity plummeted very low to the point by our own will on the brink of inevitable annihilation. This was a time in antiquity when God was described as being forceful with wrath and vengeance. Thus the earth was cleansed of its wickedness to renew the earth with people who could evolve with the LORD's favor. From what God disclosed to me in visions, I can only reason that God showed His authority through force only because humankind plummeted so deep into corruption that there was no other way to save us from our extinction. The foul choices of people lead them to continually commit atrocious crimes of wickedness against one another. God was in the position of either interfering with our free will or permitting us to annihilate the whole human race. The scarcity of God's intervention only proves to me that God wants us to survive and cares about our outcome while extremely respecting our own will.

Fortunately some of us learn through our mistakes. Others remain blind and are clueless to consequences. I understood that only those who deliberately choose to rebel God's ways of righteousness, peace, and a loving nature would fall all the way down to destruction. They will reap destruction because they sow destruction. The rest of us who continue to seek the path of goodness and sincerely ask for forgiveness will continue to evolve and navigate through the trials and life lessons as God tries to steer us home. God's ultimate goal was for us to evolve in love for one another and obtain good virtues to lead our lives into peace. This is how I can reason why the Old Testament describes our Creator in a way that is contrary to what I witnessed. I see too many valuable lessons in the Old Testament to toss any of it away, even though I can't conceive of our Creator as being vengeful or jealous. But was this Old Testament description contrary to a God of perfection when men were *always* wicked?

This explains the need why there is a time for all things, even a time for war and a time for peace, a time for destroying and a time for rebuilding. But in the time when people are not always wicked, then there is no need for destroying or forcing submission through discipline or punishment because there is the hope of learning and repentance. Jesus came as a visual and physical example of God's love, mercy and forgiveness as he taught salvation through repentance. Thus the message of Christ sets all people free from the bondage to sin. Now I understand how the Old and the New Testaments were both essential and united in purpose.

I pray that there are enough people who heed warnings and I hope that these revelations and lessons that I've shared will lead more people to the salvation of our human race.

Chapter Twelve

Sin and Free Will

To understand how humankind came to know sin is parallel to the story about Adam and Eve, the first man and woman described in the Bible. Through this vision my mind melded in the spirit with the thoughts of the first man and woman so that I may understand what happened before they came to Earth. In the spirit, we have access to experience the past, present and future events because time is not limited like it is in the manifested world. Time and space came into existence when Creation began as described in chapter four.

The first man and woman lived in the presence of God in a higher spiritual realm, and their spirits were free, safe and innocent. We were naive spiritual entities before we were manifested in the flesh. While we were existing in God's direct presence, we interacted with God with direct communication. We were not omniscient because we were spiritual entities without being able to think completely on our own without the influence from God's presence. Our soul did not have any evil inclinations in the spirit and we were close to God just as children live with their parents. No distance was felt between us. We were created to live in God's presence with love and peace. We were lavished with everything we could possibly need.

Then in my vision, I perceived God remembering and acknowledging that we were to use our own free will to explore our own opinions and to make life choices. We couldn't continue to be directly tutored by God on how to live our lives if we were to have our own will. God wanted us to choose to love the ways of the divine nature but it was our choice to choose our destiny. We were not forced to love God. Forced love was not pure and it didn't really mean anything of importance if it wasn't chosen from our own will. God wanted us to experience a way of life that was of our own making.

Even though God's love wasn't forced on us while we lived in a heightened manifested realm (before having a physical body on earth), we were continually aware of God's presence. Therefore, we couldn't freely *choose* to live in God's direct presence while we had no other option but that in that realm. That realm permeated with an awareness of God's eternal presence and love for us which influenced our thoughts. We always felt loved, cherished and secure. If we were always aware of God then this presence wasn't necessarily our choice. In addition to the gift of free will, God also chose to give us eternal life because God wanted to be loved and to share abundant love with us forever. That love was different from any love that I know on earth. There are no restrictions to separate us from the love of God. Only while we live in distant realms away from our awareness of God's presence may we feel distanced, even though God's love for us still remains, only hidden.

Unfortunately, there are two things which pull us away from God . . . rebellion and the corruption of our spirit. God had warned the first spiritual man and woman not to taste the *fruit* that would lead them astray or they would suffer death, but they did not understand what death was. Through this vision, I could *feel* what they thought and felt. They could not understand about consequences about anything that wasn't in line with divinity. In their mind, what could possibly be beyond divinity? What was death?

As long as they stayed harmoniously with God they had a blissful

Sin and Free Will

life, but the farther they migrated away from God, the more difficult their life would be. But what would it be like to have a more difficult life? They had not experienced anything that was difficult.

If you can recall, sin did not exist in the very beginning, but the possibility of sin became manifested during the process to give humankind free will and eternal life. In order to have free will is to permit the possibility of dissension, but it was a choice. We didn't have to sin. We could form our own opinions which opened the chance for discord because we were not all-knowing of wisdom as God is. Therefore, the "tree" of the knowledge of good and evil appeared in the garden[59] but its fruit was not ever tasted by humankind yet. (Again, this analogy was written in a language that people may understand through symbolism.)

The first man and woman were innocent of wrongdoing and they didn't even think to do any harm. God protected them and they lived in innocence without the awareness of harm. They didn't question God or divine guidance. God was like a perfect protective parent who guided them with the proper way to live in peace and bliss. God spoke and they listened, they submitted to God without question even if they didn't understand everything. They knew without a doubt that God's way was always the best way. Everything was peaceful and in harmony. There was nothing to dislike or to bring discord.

So when the *tree* that presented a *choice* between good and evil appeared in the spiritual garden, the tree of eternal life also appeared. If and when the man and woman chose to explore to learn about the contrast of goodness versus evil, they would be sent out from the realm of perfection to explore a realm of contrasts. Our spiritual entity would then be clothed with a mortal body to permit us to experience an illusion of separation.

It states in the Bible that Adam and Eve were barred from the tree of eternal life and forced to leave the Garden of Paradise. We had to leave before we had the opportunity to taste the fruit of eternal life while we explored the earth's realm of polarity, or evil would remain with us for eternity. God had a plan to use the lessons of good and evil along with divine assistance and guidance to bring us back home without allowing sin to endure forever. God wanted us to leave behind the evil that pulled us away. Besides, that would go against the mirroring process of God reflecting invisible attributes through Creation because there is no evil in God, so evil cannot be eternal. God is perfection. God knew all things with a perfect understanding of balance between complimentary natures. Our goal was to find this balance and avoid harmful things of whatever kind.

In the physically manifested form of Creation, our world would project a polarization of God's attributes to the extreme degree. Our world would pull perfection (which was the balance between complimentary natures) into two opposite directions as in the ying-yang, darkness and light. (This made sense to me as I recalled the experience when there was no form before the Creation process began. I only perceived a static state of light and dark commingling as one.)

To temporarily block the first man and woman from the tree of eternal life, they would have to leave the garden of Eden (Kingdom of God) without tasting the fruit of eternal life. This is why people became mortal in the fleshly state. Even though our soul is eternal, our physical body was a temporary vessel which held us bound to the earth's realm. Earth is a place where we could learn through the polarity of all the extreme natures between good and evil, ie: positive and negative energies, lightness and darkness, etc.

If we seek the divine nature of the 'good fruit,' we would reconnect with an eternal bonding back into the Kingdom of God. Our primary purpose in life is to bridge the abyss of separation back in communion with God. If we seek the nature that was of the 'bad fruit,' we would descend

Sin and Free Will

away from our connection with God and possibly disengage our lifeline as a member of God's Kingdom. We would be as the prodigal son who recklessly lived our lives until we learned to do better, or we would descend toward destruction and away from the divinity of perfection. All-in-all, we were given the choice to migrate toward the realm where our individual life energy resonated with like energy. We may belong anywhere between the extreme light and the extreme darkness. It was up to us as to how bright or how dark we chose for our destiny.

In a polarized world, we have the freedom to migrate toward perfection or to fall away. The first man and woman had lived in bliss and never felt pain before their separation from God's Kingdom, so they couldn't conceive of what the opposite of perfection would be like. I felt their thoughts as they chose of their free will to taste the fruit of good and evil because temptation was aroused by a curiosity (not a snake--that's symbolism). They wanted to know God better by finding out what wasn't perfection. To find that which is not perfection is to experience a separation from perfection. The first man and woman were curious to find out what God wasn't, which lead humankind away from God, but it was really for the primal mission to find out what God *is* and the difference between us.

This explanation is not my own doing. I learned this while my mind was carried along by the Holy Spirit[60] and as I reflect on it, this really makes sense to me. Adam and Eve were not evil and they did not sin by wanting to explore about "good and evil". This was inevitable and part of the process to teach us about life. They had honorable intentions to more fully know God. They greatly loved and respected God, but they had no idea about the difficult things they could experience in this world. This is a little twist in understanding that I had not considered before and I can empathize with them. It makes more sense to me than the idea that Adam and Eve were being punished because they ate a piece of tempting fruit from a tree that God warned them not to eat. Why have such a temptation if it might cause us to sin? That's such a horrible trick! But understanding why such a choice became available makes much more sense.

In the state of not knowing who we are, and discovering life as it unfolds, we could question what we did not understand. We could experience what happens when we chose such and such, etc. The first man and woman had lived in perfect love and freedom in the presence of God, but they had a curiosity to know who they were and how they differed from God and everything else. Because their state of naive innocence didn't know where the knowledge of good and evil would lead them, they freely chose to find out. They had to independantly experience a life of tribulations in order to understand and appreciate a Kingdom that God wanted to provide for us with an existence without tribulations and pain. They had to witness and feel the effects of harmful things in order to freely choose to reject it. How could they reject evil (harmful things) if they didn't know what it was or how it affected life? When they ate from the tree of the knowledge of good and evil, they accepted to *know* the fruit of good and evil in all of its manifestations. We set out on a road to find out.

Since God wanted us to choose righteous behavior of our own volition, God allowed us to find out what the realm of good and evil contained. The negative consequences of our choices would help us understand why goodness is preferable. God didn't want us to suffer the negative consequences and so He gave us warnings through divine guidance. Unfortunately with freedom, we also have the freedom to go against God's warning and rebel this guidance. People may choose their own destiny by ignoring God's goal for humanity, even though God had a higher destiny for us in mind.

We weren't forced to evolve in the spirit, but when we part from God's divine nature, this places a distance between us and God because we are leaving perfection. It wasn't until after the first humans tasted the fruit that they realized how dreadfully wrong their choice was. Their new polarized world grew thorns and thistles and they had to work by the sweat of their brow. They were no longer just given what they wanted and needed. They experienced pain for the first time with all the difficulties of life and consequences. This is how they descended into sin. They immediately felt how drastically different life was without having awareness of God's constant presence and I felt that they constantly mourned their decision, making their life on earth unbearable while retaining their prior memories of Heaven. Guilt set in.

Just as the first man and woman, our soul had already lived and interacted with God in a higher realm of light. How could people live on earth to make our own choices without our memory of God to learn everything from the root upward? A veil was placed over our minds to conceal our memory of our prior state, of God and Heaven. God's presence was hidden from us and we had amnesia of our former self. I can imagine that their hearts must have felt crushed if they retained all of their memories of their prior state. I can empathize with them because I have a little taste of that pain myself because I recovered some of my pre-birth memories of heaven. I remember living in that realm before being born on earth. I understand why everyone's memory needed to be veiled so that they could explore their life lessons on earth to freely choose their own destiny.

Now people have the responsibility to make choices and reap the consequences, good or bad as lessons learned. If humankind felt the consequences of wrong choices, would we return to follow God's path? Would we forsake evil to find all that is good? Some of our choices would be in contradiction to perfection, but surely all of humankind would not intentionally choose to be always evil. Surely all of us would not seek pain and destruction and not want our lives to change for the better. Surely all of humankind would not reject God and the loving nature of divinity. But we could not turn back until we had learned from our own life experiences from the consequences of the knowledge of good and evil. Humankind had to experience an existence which felt separated from God so that we could compare it with the joy of our prior existence that was aware of God's presence. We all had to experience loneliness and sorrow in place of wholeness and bliss. Therefore, to know an existence without an awareness of God's direct presence, and still freely choose to live a righteous life of divine attributes would make us even more precious to God! This would prove that our heart was in harmony with God because our spirit would be attracted to the nature of divinity. We would choose to evolve toward perfection of our soul and our destiny would be the fruit of *our* labor. This is the highest goal of life on earth.

In the heavenly realm, our heavenly body lived in freedom without any confinement. We were free to go wherever we wished without danger. Now, living on a physical realm, humankind would have to be confined, restricted and limited in our earthly body. God had to clothe our heavenly bodies with skins of mortal flesh. Our material body would keep our individual soul drawn to the earth like a magnet, where we could not escape until we had overcome the trials of the earth life. And, to *know* knowledge, man must touch, see, and hear all things from its root. We had to begin to live *without* the direct presence of God's nourishing directives in order for us to be responsible for our own destiny. We become what we choose to become.

The realm of earth is polarized. It's a realm of the essence of God stretched out into reciprocal counter essences. To live in a world of polarity would take us through very difficult trials and tribulations. We must overcome ignorance by finding knowledge. To find knowledge we need to discover truth in all of its myriad of manifestations. This knowledge of truth will lead us into an understanding of all things and free us from the pull of sin. The more we learn, the more we reflect intellect and wisdom. The more we reflect a balanced state of morality, the more we become attuned to God's frequency where we become aware of God through a spiritual connection. If we draw from deep within our heart, we still can find a connection back to God. The spirit will help us to remember. When we are open to a higher conscience, heightened knowledge is revealed through the veil as enlightenment.

The dilemma though about this veil, is that we have no knowledge of God and the heavenly realm while we are confined to the earth without someone or something to inform us to search for it. We do not know God nor do we know the truth until we find it. God remedied this by sending the *Living Word* to instruct us through messengers so that we could come to discover God. Signs, miracles, and representatives were sent in different forms to bring awareness of God. No matter how God chose to reveal to us, the domain of the earth's negative pull of deception (veiled from the truth) had control over us as long as *we* permitted the ways of ignorance and deception to dominate our hearts. We had difficulty finding God because we didn't understand God's ways. In ignorance, we made choices which lead us to migrate away from God.

For us to win back our true home in the heavenly realm, we cannot want to sin. Sin is in opposition to divinity and does not exist in Heaven and cannot be there. To conquer sin, we must be drawn to God, desire to find and to live closer in God's presence. We need to become incorporated with the divine essence without the reciprocal counterpart which is destructive of positive energy. God is to be found by people who seek in spirit and in truth. We must break away from the desires that pull us away from God. When we live in righteousness, forsaking all evil and turning away from harmful ways, then we overcome negative impulses. When our material body dies on this earth, our true self (our higher self) will return to God because we belong to God from the beginning.[61] If our life energy harmonizes with the Divine Light energy, then we will stay in the realm of light as a permanent member of God's Kingdom.

If we have not learned our lessons of the knowledge of good and evil by the time our physical body dies, then God will place us where we need to be[62] to learn the lessons we are lacking to bring us into knowledge. We will begin a renewed life, again without the knowledge of our previous existence. How do you suppose that this can be true? Pay close attention to the following scriptures that men want to disregard: *"I tell you this: the present generation will live to see it all."*[63] That verse was written nearly two thousand years ago! How can that generation live to see it all if we don't have multiple life experiences on earth? Also, *"you are also my witnesses, because you have been with me from the first."*[64] But *how* can we be from the first unless it is referring to our higher self who once lived with God? *"A vessel he was making out of clay would be spoilt in his hands, and then he would start again and mould it into another vessel to his liking. Then the word of the Lord came to me: 'Can I not deal with you, Israel, says the Lord, as the potter deals with his clay? You are clay in my hands like the clay in his.'"*[65] Do you think that when we die, then we will go to heaven in a state of death? God is not the God of the dead, but of the living![66] Our life force is alive and can be renewed and placed inside multiple vessels.

If we had complete memory of Heaven during our state on earth, we could not stand to stay on earth because we would constantly mourn the bliss of Heaven and reject our grueling lessons on earth. We long to feel happiness and freedom instead of sadness and confinement. Don't you feel that deep within you? Where does this yearning for freedom, love and happiness come from? This is why people seek companionship and self expression. The memory of Heaven would weigh our hearts down with great sorrow and mourning if it wasn't veiled in our present state. We would most likely refuse to live in the earth's realm to avoid going through the trials of pain and tribulations, for nobody enjoys being hurt and struggling to survive. We have to go through pain in our lives, because we *chose* to learn its contents. When we begin each new life, we take with us the lessons that we had previously learned through the interpolation of positive and negative influences in our lives.

You may think that you would not have personally chose to learn the polarizing effects of good and evil and may wish to blame the first man and woman for this choice for all humankind, but from the beginning of creation, humankind had the inclination to learn all things. It was the goal of humankind to learn and evolve in spirit to overcome ignorance. They didn't know what evil was and so we cannot say that we would not have made the same choices as Adam and Eve had, because we are now in a different state of mind where we do feel, see and experience evil. When we never experienced evil, we wouldn't have had a reason to stay away from it and we wouldn't have feared it. We had no sense of fear in Heaven.

To learn is good and God wants us to learn, yet also wants to protect us from the pain of this earth and encouraged us to avoid sin. We needed to learn as much as possible from God before we came to live in the realm of earth. That is why God only warned us to stay away from the tree of the knowledge of good and evil but did not prevent us from choosing it. That was our choice as well. We were destined to learn from life and so it was inevitable that humankind would sooner or later choose to discover the contents of the knowledge of good and evil.

We cannot see where we are being led in our future. God is in control of life and guides us where we need to go for the good and for the advancement of our soul. But, unfortunately, some people have lost faith in

God and have forsaken Him. God repeatedly showed love and guidance to humankind, but many continued to choose away from God out of ignorance. They rejected God before discovering God. This is why God took pity on us and sent the beloved Son (God's clear image of reflection) to give us a visual example to follow in our very presence on earth.[67]

Those people who do win their escape from the earth's domain have learned their lessons to overcome evil. They will not have to come to earth again unless they choose to come to help other people evolve. If they come to earth to help humankind, they may return to God. Jesus is one who accepted to come to earth from above to help people defeat the earth's domain. He fulfilled a mission and lives in the presence of God until he chooses to return again when the time ripens for it and God sends him. If only humankind would learn to truly seek God of our own volition, but it is written that God will send the Messiah again.

The purpose of his mission when Jesus came over 2000 years ago was to show humankind how to seek God and hopefully choose to live in the ways of righteousness. But, before God sent Jesus to teach us and to bring us to salvation, people were encouraged to learn from previous methods in gradual steps in hopes that we would return to God without needing to send the Son. Nevertheless, humankind still continued to turn away. God knows us so well and already foresaw what we might do, so prepared in advance to send God's image in human form (the very likeness of God's invisible character through Christ, the annointed) into the world. It was revealed that God would send us Christ (the khristos). God's Word reveals His foreknowledge of our development from the days of old and up to the present. The past reveals the present and the present reflects the past. In this way, God's Word testifies to God's foreknowledge. It is to our own benefit that we should study the life lessons contained in scripture, such as . . .

Noah was the last of his generation who held onto his faith in God. Once Noah was gone, humankind would be doomed without assistance because nobody else sought God's guidance. There would be none left to keep the channel (the plumb line) connected to God. So God told Noah to build a giant ark for the purpose to rebuild humanity from the foundation of earth again. Noah was tested to see if he had the fortitude and obedience to trust God. The rest of Noah's neighbors ridiculed and taunted Noah for building an ark on dry land.

Noah's ark was symbolic of the Ark of the Covenant which was to be given to humanity through Moses. Noah's ark was covered with pitch inside and out to keep the boat afloat and secure it from sinking into ultimate destruction. Just as Noah's ark, the Ark of the Covenant was plated inside and out with gold to symbolize a shield of purity to keep humanity from sinking all the way down into the depths of depravity. This is also in reference to when Jesus said to wash the inside of the cup and then the outside would also be clean, referring to ourselves.

Noah's ark held the precious cargo of man, two by two, male and female, (and all of the assembled creatures), to restore and repopulate the earth with the hope of renewed faith in God. With so many people gone astray, there were too many evil influences which choked any possible progress. The tender young shoots were choked by the weeds and they couldn't reach the light. Therefore, people needed a new beginning without the strength of evil influence being so prevalent. God sent the rains to wash away our sins and humankind was given another chance and repopulated the earth. We still had to go through the process of learning through the extremes of "good and evil". We were given another chance of a renewed life, which was also the purpose of sending Christ.[68] God promised not to flood the entire earth again and set a bow as a symbol of this promise.

Chapter Thirteen

A Universal Religion
Part A

I understood from the vision about religion that the Old Testament needs to be brought together with the New Testament into a deeper, interlinking understanding. There is a deeper significance about the Original Tablets in which Moses threw down and broke into pieces. The first Tablets that God gave to Moses, (written from God's own hand), was too vast, too compound and intricate for people to understand. I can understand this because the revelations that I received were multi-faceted and spread out in multiple directions at the same time. Therefore, the Tablets were broken into smaller shards of information. God replaced the Tablets and then asked Moses to chisel them (into his understanding), to give the Torah to all the people. The Torah is the milk of God's Word. We were not ready to eat solid food.[69]

Now is the time to wean people from their misconceptions and explain how the Old and New Testaments support each other, just as Judaism and Christianity should support each other. The revelations that I was given also supports all of the testimonies from all of the prophets within the Bible as well as those from other branches of religion. This also includes those who have testified to their own spiritually transformative experiences and near-death experiences; of which they have become witnesses from above. We are all connected to the same foundation of life through the spirit.

It is clear to me that there are truths revealed in all divinely inspired religions, while at the same time, they each have their own deviations and distortions which came about through their followers. All people are essentially equal in essence and we each have our purpose and fellowship to the broader humanity. Each of us is a piece of a grander picture.

To generally place any group of people above all of the others is to be lead by arrogance, pride and ego. Their focus is for self rather than all. These attitudes then give birth to prejudice, bigotry, and oppression because arrogant people strive for superiority. This leads men into conflict and war. When groups of people divide against each other, then humankind falls into ruin. Just as a divided kingdom falls, as long as armies fight to suppress the rest of humankind then destruction of the human race will follow. As long as people infringe on the rights of others and the selfish, arrogant leaders fight to force people to serve them, then they are set upon a world of violence and war which will not be conquered by their aggression. People will always resist oppression as long as they are able to do so because the nature of the spirit is freedom. Tyrants try to wipe out dialogue and resistance to oppression. If people dare to speak up about their abuse, the tyrant uses genocide. So I ask, do not be as one who cannot see the light of unity. Only mutual respect for each other begets harmony and peace.

Unity does not mean that all people must turn into clones. We weren't created in diversity to fight for the top position and then force the remaining human race to be chameleons. Most people will judge in ignorance what they don't understand. They form human opinion and speculation based on their own thoughts and bias. A person who has bias will see diversity as a threat and then choose to be unyielding to different ideas or new discoveries that they hadn't discovered for themselves. Bias forms resistance to change which in turn leads to prejudice and intolerance of diversity. Intolerant people want to destroy anything that is different from their own culture and belief system. This leads to a world of conflict.

An aside, this is why it is difficult for God's servants to carry the torch throughout the world, and yet they do it to help humanity evolve past our human boundaries. The light needs to pierce the darkness and then radiate outwards to expand the human mind. This opens the door to the upper realm. Without light then the door remains hidden and makes it all the more difficult to evolve in the spirit.

A person who is not biased will embrace diversity without resistance. They are open to dialogue and can adapt when they understand the need for change. There is unity in diversity when people live by the unity of the heart. The light of God's truth radiates out through all things in diversity if you will contemplate on what spiritual unity means without bias. Unity of conscience should be able to reason what works and what does not work for society. As society evolves then there must be room for change. If we truly want our world to become universally peaceful, then we must remove the prejudice and bigotry that was handed down through our predecessors. We need to accept that our world was created in diversity, not for us to hate diversity, but to embrace it. It is not God's will to lose anyone, no matter what nation, religion, ethnic makeup, gender, or anything else to fall away into spiritual depravity. If any people do fall into depravity, it is because those people freely choose to follow that path. We have all had warnings all around us which guided us to stay on the upright path. We all know that love, truth, compassion, charity, humility, self control, mercy, etc. are virtues along the upright path. How many of us follow down the opposite path of hate, deception, oppression, greed, arrogance, tyranny, murder, etc? There is a better way to live our lives which invokes peace, but we must choose it.

I intend to reveal to the nations an existence of life lived in peace, a renewed world living together as one, and embracing each other with better understanding. If the whole of humankind would like to see this happen, God is still showing the way. God loves us so completely and so perfectly that messengers are sent out into the world to bring understanding to help humanity. Do not reject the messenger without examining their message to see if it could lead to peace. Doesn't it make sense that our world could become peaceful if we just embraced diversity? Think about it.

The world was created in love and for love. Love is of God and love gives life. Violence, on the other hand, is detrimental to life. If our outlook has not love for one another, then the heart is lead with its opposite inclination of hatred for one another. Hate leads to death and destruction -- a consequence of intolerance. When there are obstacles to separate our self from loving ways, then we are blocked from the tree of eternal life. We need to transcend those obstacles.

Fortunately, hatred born of prejudice can be transformed into love if people seek change. This very book set before you is the key to unlocking some of God's mysteries. Why else would I have received all of this information if not to share these divine truths to help transform our world for the better? I can't transform the world all by myself. This has to be a joint effort and there has to be a starting point open to change.

My wish is to inspire others to seek God with all of their heart, mind, and soul so that more minds may be renewed with the Divine Spirit of Truth. I want to point out so much scripture to support what I say because I want others to see that what I share has already been shared in scripture, but truly each person needs to search for theirself. It was there all along. We just needed to see with new perception. If you find any information or guidance that I've shared which doesn't agree with you, then try to reason out whether your viewpoint is coming from an unbiased and broader perspective of love. Don't change scripture to suit your bias, but transform your perspective into an all-inclusive interpretation. It all begins within the heart.

Reflect on your own interpretation of religion and see if your rights would be violated if someone outside of your religion felt as you do within their own religion. Evaluate what you would feel if that person felt the same way in reverse. See how others would treat you if they did as you do to them. If you harbor ill will toward people of another religious faith, then how would you feel if they harbored the same feelings toward you based solely on their religious bigotry? So few people examine their own hypocrisy. They want other people to be tolerant of their beliefs while they don't do the same in reverse. When people hate and rebuke those people who reflect kindness and the nature of divinity, little do they realize that they are setting up their own future which is in enmity with divinity. Their future will come back to bite them with the same negative energy that they are now sowing. In all things, think about where you are leading yourself in the future through the living mirror of self reflection. Use your conscience to guide your own life and keep what is good and avoid what is harmful for you as well as for others. Each person is responsible for the choices they make in their own life. Let life be what it may and seek to enlighten others in the ways of a universal perspective. May our world be renewed with a heightened understanding to live together in harmony and begin again.

Part B

Now, getting back on the subject of the guidance given to Moses. Moses wanted to see God but was only permitted to see the back side of God.[70] This was symbolic to indicate that God's fullness needed to be hidden from us on earth. Exodus 33:19 says, *"I will make <u>all</u> my <u>character</u>*

pass before you." Thus, God wants us to *know* His character, but reveals this in portions of limited insight and through the nature of the spirit.

Likewise, God's Word which was given to humankind at that time, had to be veiled. Our limited knowledge could not contain the fullness of God's multifaceted guidance because it was too complicated for us to comprehend. (Divine Truth is infinite in knowledge while our physical mind is limited in understanding.) God planned for the Word to be given by increments and used it that way for a good purpose. Moses broke the tablets as a symbol of God's Truth being broken into little shards of information that people could handle because our realm is a reflection of God's revealing nature. This shattered Tablet that Moses broke is like the shattered mirror of the Creation process that was used to reflect the nature of divinity into smaller proportions within each being.

That is why there are so many different religions. All religions have truth, but only a shard of the mirror. Each is a microcosm of the enlarged divine Tablet. Unfortunately, the various religions as they are today had not remained pure and clear but have become distorted by incorrect human perceptions. There are added-on concepts and missing pieces of information which have been forgotten, not handed down, and worn away by time. They have morphed into a reflection of human interpretations.

All religions cannot be brought back together as a whole according to God's Original Tablets as they now stand. If one were to try to fit the shattered pieces back together as they are now, the mirror would not resemble the Original mirror of Divine reflection. God had a better plan to use the pieces in a different way. God revealed to me that He doesn't discard anything that was given to us for good. The parts within all religions which were followed correctly could be grafted back as a scion into the original Word. This is why all religions need to go through a universal restoration.

God gave Moses two tablets written with the finger of God. They were the handiwork of God, and the writing was God's writing; engraved on both sides.[71] After the tablets were broken into pieces, God replaced them and told Moses to do the chiseling and to write on the tablets *like* the words which were on the first tablets. The replaced tablets contained the Ten Words that God wrote, and the 'words of the covenant' that Moses wrote which contained God's covenant.[72] This indicates that Moses interpreted God's original words into his written language which were engraved on both sides of the original two tablets. (Then these 'words of the covenant' were later isolated into 613 separate commandments written by ancient rabbis and teachers of the law.)

In addition to the written scriptures, they also had the Talmud. The Talmud is a collection of the Jewish Oral laws, called the Mishnah, and the commentaries of the rabbis, called the Gemara. The Talmud was not handed down to Christianity, but was kept within the Jewish sect -- mainly, because they were not finished interpreting the oral laws until after the destruction of the first temple.

How did God use all of the different religions for a good purpose?

Each group of people formed their belief as they could understand their piece of God's Word. They then formed their own branch of 'religion' and defined their understanding according to what their prophet received. The problem was that the people did not focus on religion with the correct focus in their hearts as they studied scripture. People viewed religion through a narrow-minded, exclusive perspective. They dominated over religion with their human interpretation of scriptures and resisted the diversity of God's divine guidance. Religion became a battlefield of diversified sects instead of realizing the universal unity of each shard coming from the same original divine Source.

People were supposed to evolve in understanding through the spirit of love and tolerance until they could embrace another shard of knowledge. If our hearts were in the right place we would have learned from each other instead of fighting against each other. The Ark of the Covenant is symbolic of this.[73] The Ark was plated inside and out with gold, which is symbolic of purity. The covenant means that each person needs to become spiritually pure, inside and out with goodness. The Ark held all of the broken pieces of the original Tablets which Moses broke. This is symbolic that each person needs to embrace each shard of religion within themselves. The gold jar of manna represents the bread which comes down from Heaven and into a human vessel. The bread symbolizes the down-pouring of divine guidance which nourishes us with the pure Living Word within. The staff of Aaron represents the rod of God, the straight path of justice which blooms and helps us to prosper in the spirit. Above the Ark are the cherubim of God's glory which also represents our highest destiny in God's presence, and where earth reflects Heaven.

Instead, so many people became biased toward their own shard of 'religion' which incorporated their own self-centered, narrow viewpoints. They were taught to fear apostasy without really understanding what it meant from a broader perspective. Even though scriptures explain that God wants to save all people in every nation[74] we still became bigoted against diverse peoples and religions instead of embracing our diversity. This was because of our focus on ourselves and our own community instead of the greater humanity. People were permitted to continue in their ways in hopes that they would eventually learn from their mistakes. Unfortunately, instead of learning through our mistakes, many people grew hard in their hearts and developed hatred and bigotry which led them into religious battles to the extent that the people massacred other people because of their religions[75] thus leading humankind toward destruction.

For people to understand knowledge from its root, they must reap what they sow. They must experience what they project onto others. God helped the people along who were following the right path as they were able. In this way, many people transcended religious prejudice and respected the freedom of religious diversity. If people continue to be coerced into resisting diversity, then they are no longer free to pursue the right path. The only way for people to see their errors is for them to suffer the consequences of their actions. We must feel, see and hear consequences so that we can understand what our choices do. How long do they need to kill one another until they open their eyes to see?

The people who have the correct focus toward religion will discover the mystery of God's Living Word and will grow in understanding the spirit as long as they are free to do so. They will grow in religious tolerance and will be able to live in peace with a life filled with blessings.

Those who are intolerant of religious diversity will continue to suffer from their actions of bigotry and hate as God's Word would stay confounded to them. This process was helpful to weed out those good 'fish' from the stubborn 'fish', or the wheat from the chaff. Those who didn't have the seed for spiritual growth would spiral downward toward darkness and destruction as long as they refused to turn toward God in spirit. It is time for all religions to be re-examined and sifted through a universal sieve to separate the rightly guided from the corrupted teachings.

The worst interpretations among the religions will be clearly identified by their ruthless actions of spreading havoc and violence throughout the world. Their corrupt interpretations have come to a head and needs to be plucked out and reformed. If those who adhere to the rightly guided teachings do nothing to weed them out, then corruption will continue to grow and multiply until life on earth becomes unbearable. Sooner or later people will discover that they must do something to stop the spreading of destructive energy from ruining society as it becomes a matter of survival of the whole human race. Then the stubborn people who did not evolve upward for one reason or another will be dealt with as needed according to God's plan.

I saw in my visions that God's love was there all along for every nation and every person. There are miraculous events which took place in each of the religions. God has chosen people from all nations, all religions, and all ethnic backgrounds. All of God's prophets and messengers were devoted to God's will. God would not have chosen them if their intentions in the heart were different from God's will.

Most people weren't open to learn about other scriptures from other prophets because they were resistant to learning from any other people. Why? Because they believed that they were superior and set apart from other people. Their arrogant attitudes lead them astray. When they did find out about other prophets in other lands, most people did not inquire into the other religions as they should have with a tolerant heart. Their intolerance intensified because the people were lead by self absorption of their own traditions and interpretations of their own shard of religion. Selfish pride, arrogance and vanity corrupted them as a result of their ignorance of God's all-embracing ways.

People were also afraid to explore into another religion for fear of being mislead. Why should they fear being mislead if they didn't at first feel that the other religion was inferior to theirs? They didn't even attempt to understand the other religions well enough to judge them. Little did they know that they were already mislead by their own prejudice in their heart. This is why scripture warns us to guard our heart more than any treasure.

A Universal Religion

This is where our actions take root. Many people couldn't fathom the possibility of finding truth in the other branches of religion even when we are all branches of the same tree! A tree of unity has the same roots in the same Source. God, whatever name we call the Source, our Creater, by our own terminology and language, is the Founder of us all. If monotheists think that other groups of people in other religions follow another god, then this indicates that they do not truly believe in one God as they say they do. How can there be another God if there is only one? Bigoted people seek to destroy the other limbs of the tree because their hearts do not recognize the connection and importance of all branches. They see religion and humanity with narrow vision and can't expand to see more than one branch, encompassing the whole tree. God's original Faith is universal in the spirit of the divine heart. It is inclusive toward the unity of all humankind. It embraces the diversity of Creation and does not try to destroy that which brings beauty and harmony to life.

Shine The Light

Original Tablet written by the Hand of God ------ The Original True Faith	God's Divine guidance was far too complicated for humankind to understand, therefore it was broken into smaller proportions and given to us in fragments. Each shard was given to a different prophet from different nations, which then became diverse religions.	If each shard of religion was kept clear and was understood in the proper way, God had hoped that they could be reunited. But, placing the pieces back together now will only reveal crevices and missing pieces. It no longer reflects the Original Tablet.

Jesus and his disciples, and all of God's prophets and witnesses were chosen by God to guide people to understand His Word at the rate in which humankind could handle. God did not want to break our vessel so He broke His Original Tablets into smaller proportions of information. The second tablets which were chiseled out by Moses was translated into an interpretation that humankind could contemplate. People were supposed to gather each shard of the Original Tablet within ourselves as our understanding increased. God would wait patiently for each person who freely chose to learn more. As a person reached a certain level of understanding, God would reveal additional guidance by increments, except only a few people ever evolved enough to handle more than one shard. Instead, we chose to fight against one another and stay apart, which stagnated our spiritual growth and God wasn't able to guide us into deeper understanding.

A Universal Religion

Somehow with the development of each new denomination of religion, people tended to think that anyone who did not conform to their own religious views were unbelievers and enemies of God. Who is to say that their religious views were correct? Actually, *they* were the ones who were lead in their hearts with wicked thoughts because they vehemently and aggressively killed over their differences of opinions and views of faith. They followed the negative path. Their aggressive nature overcame their sense of reason and they fell astray from love. They did not learn from one another to suppress their violent tendencies. Instead, they harbored anger and violence, forcing others against their will into their segregated religion, punishable upon death! It has never been their right to judge other people in matters of faith[76] Why would an all-powerful God need our help to destroy what was created? God could do that in a heartbeat if that's what God wanted. Can you see that these human tendencies were not God centered? This bigoted attitude did not lead us toward peace and it never will. Those who deliberately seek to destroy others will be destroyed themselves. What we do to others will come back to us, and this is exactly why wars continue!

If people were lead by God's qualities of love, patience, compassion, and mercy, then these wars claimed to be fought in the name of God would not have happened. God does not murder people or force anyone against their will to believe what they cannot accept. Free will was one of God's wishes for humankind, but men misused it to harm one another. Again and again, God guided us to live in good will. If we continue to repel away from divinity, then by our own deliberate choice, we will descend toward destruction because that's the consequence of rebelling against good will and migrating towards negative inclinations.

If these adherents to a violent interpretation of religion won't stop their perpetual violence and killing, they will continue to destroy all of the human race. I was shown in a vision that those who follow the path of destruction won't stop killing until their interpretation of religion was the only one left standing. But at what cost? Millions upon millions of people would be murdered until these vile, corrupt people will finally see that it was *they* who were in error! Their way of stamping out diversity would end up with only one man standing because they would continue destroying until only one human remained. There are differences of opinion between just two people! God revealed to me that if we don't stop them in their destructive tracks, they will destroy God's Creation of the whole human race! This was how wicked people had become in the days of Noah and why God sent a flood to wipe out the wickedness of humankind. How can some people become so vile and wicked again! How have people plummeted into such depravity and moral corruption that they do not see what they do!

To preserve the human race, we must do something to transform the heart of violent people. We don't want to perpetuate their actions of violence or just put them into prisons which does not transform them. We need to find the root of what caused them to choose a destructive path. This book is my attempt to do my part for humanity. I offer to share what the Holy Spirit revealed to me in hope that enough people will read, study and heed the warnings and guidance that I was given to share. No matter how many times I try to explain in each chapter, I worry that people still may not understand what I'm trying to explain.

If people's hearts were on the right path, they would discover that there are many similarities in the core of each religion but with diverse explanations of the same truth. Along the way, some people were caught by the delusion perpetrated by human understanding which pivoted men against men. They viewed religion from inside a biased box rather than from an overlay of a universal perspective. If the consensus of humankind

A Universal Religion

would evolve into this universal perspective, they can come to an understanding for the reason why God inspired diversity in religion. It was a trial to test the nature of our heart.

Some people prefer a more energetic spiritual religion, while others prefer a more structured, stoic and disciplined religion. Whichever way the people chose, God's guidance can be found in all religions because <u>it's a matter of the condition of the heart</u> and not the name we call it. If most people transformed themselves with a purification of the heart, then our world would indeed reflect peace, and isn't that what we all want deep down inside?

I can see that all religions have so many followers with distorted viewpoints now that it's difficult to see the same universal truth as it was originally intended. Religious belief has morphed into something different than what they began in the spirit. And yet when I read each of their scriptures, I can still see the unity which reflects within all of them. It's religious prejudice which blinds people from seeing the universal Faith. It's like the saying, people "can't see the forest because of the trees". People can't see the heart of religion because religion is diverse. Can you now see how ignorant we have been to develop religious persecution and to kill over religious diversity? Each religion is a shard of the same universal mirror! Each shard was a reflection and microcosm of the original True Faith, only reflected into diverse expressions from a multi-faceted Supreme Mind. As long as we fought to stay apart, we would never come back together to find the harmony and peace of unity of the Original Faith. The Universal Faith of the spirit was always there, but the self-focused nature of our heart blinded us from seeing with a universal view.

I'm waiting for the day when the lion will lay down with the lamb - the day when we will stop attacking the truth which is gentle and peace loving. It is the nature of bigotry which corrupts the use of religion and denigrates our spirit. Bigotry is indeed an offspring of ignorance.

What will happen next?

We were given warning that God will send an Advocate to bring clear understanding and will point out where the error of right and wrong and judgment belong.[77] This Advocate is the Holy Spirit of Truth which dwells with and in those who receive God's guidance. God wants us to build upon a strong foundation for life to endure. He wants us to build upon the rock which has already been established for us. The rock was the foundation of <u>God's Living Word</u> which is founded upon love. We are supposed to support the foundation of all things with the energy of love. Unfortunately, people inadvertently built upon destructive energy and life unfolded accordingly. Violence is founded on hate and intolerance. Do we want to continue to live a life built upon violence? I believe that humankind is still searching for the foundation of love. We can find it when we transform our hearts.

We need to build our future upon the foundation of positive energy which radiates a peaceful disposition. Mutual respect and compassion for one another is such a foundation of love. It is our responsibility to clean up the misguided teachings and correct our actions by basing all things upon God's Living Word and not just through human perception. The light of truth reflects throughout all things just as a reflection is seen throughout all the mirrors. To restore harmony to our world, we must spread God's scattered truth into every corner. This process is referred to as the 'Tikkun' in the Jewish Kabbalah. (The light of truth must spread throughout all things.)

When religion is understood with the proper perception, all things will be in alignment and in harmony with God. The future is already told in the Bible that all things will be reconciled and brought back into unity with a universal restoration. Just how long that will take, nobody knows, but we have to sow positive energy in order to reap positive blessings. Life on earth evolves into what we collectively make it through the focus that begins in our heart. It's our choice. Do you want to unite our world with the blessings of harmony and peace, or do you want to divide our world until the world is destroyed by the curses of a war-torn world? What's in your heart?

Chapter Fourteen

Divine Symbolism

I understand more clearly now how stories in the scriptures are life lessons as well as being symbolic of spiritual lessons. There are lessons within lessons that as we mature in our understanding, we can discover hidden meanings beyond the literal words.

For instance, the Ark of the Covenant held the two tablets of God's guidance and covenants. The Ark was symbolic of God's hope for us. The Ark was plated with gold on the inside as well as the outside. The covenant is about God wanting people to evolve in purity by keeping divine guidance inside our hearts and to live by it. God wants us to have a pure heart on the inside as well demonstrating a righteous life with our outward behavior. The tablets written on both sides are also a reference to this; as well as when Jesus said to wash the inside of the cup and the outside will be clean as well. There are many symbolisms throughout scripture to help people understand the ways of the spirit.

The story of the tower of Babel reflected the desire of some men that wanted to be worshipped as a god (which reflected the sin of Lucifer). The story of Sodom and Gomorrah reflected the desire to live hedonistic lives in which people forsake God and divine guidance to find transient pleasures to satisfy our own desires without thinking about the harm we may cause to others. Through those stories we are shown what could happen to us if we should choose the same. They are warnings. We can't live only for our own selfish pleasure without considering the pain we could cause to others by overlooking their welfare. We can't live for pleasure at the expense of other people's pain and misfortune. We are our own worst enemy when we forsake God and the guidance which was given to help bring us to be the best we can be. Just as those before us, we would fall all the way to ruin if we refused to pursue a virtuous life of morality and ethics. Once the last connection to God is severed, then death comes to those who may suffer the "second death". The first death is referring to the physical death of the body. The second death is referring to the spiritual death of a corrupted individual soul. Although the spirit does not die, our soul may become dormant, like being asleep, and not aware of life.

Even though we continue to rebel and cause pain, God does not stop loving us. God has always wanted to find a way to save us from our iniquities, but needed to do so in a way which reflected divine characteristics through the *living reflection*. The reflection needs to emulate God's character, and so God searched through all the hearts of humankind and found Abraham who was the last of his generation to stay strong in his faith in God. Was Abraham's faith strong enough to pass the test of personal sacrifice? God would test him to see if he would replicate the likeness of God's character enough to sacrifice his own son in the service of God. Would Abraham stay loyal to God and reflect what God was resorted to do in order to save humankind? Could Abraham give up his son who was the most precious and dear to his heart? If one person would stay committed to God, then humanity has hope because God won't give up on us. If Abraham had faith and obedience to do what God asked of him, then humankind had hope to receive salvation through God's most beloved Son. Thus, this is why Abraham was tested by being asked to sacrifice his truly beloved son.

The Bible testifies that Abraham loved Isaac more than anything else in his life *under* God. It took all of Abraham's faith to do the unthinkable. His heart must have been breaking in excruciating pain to think that he had to sacrifice his son. When God saw that Abraham was faithful and true to his commitment, then God would do the same for us and send God's anointed Son to save the people. Abraham proved to God that humankind could learn to be selfless and loyal to God.

God then replaced Isaac with a substitute offering so that Abraham's son would not suffer death. Of course God did not want Abraham to harm his son, but he was tested to prove the depth of his commitment. Because Abraham honored God before his own love for his son, he was favored by God and this gave hope of salvation to humankind. If Abraham did not reflect God's virtue of personal sacrifice, then humankind may have been doomed to sin unless God either took away our free will, since we continually misused it to harm one another, or found another way of salvation. I felt that God did not want to take away our free will, and so resorted to find a way of salvation. God's love for us is never ending and yet we continued to cause sorrow and grief when we deliberately harmed one another with injustices.

Besides helping people on earth, the scriptural stories were also symbolic of the heavenly realm for the purpose to bring divine attributes on earth. All life lessons are necessary to help us learn about God's character and depth of love. Isaac was handed over to God to serve the divine plan just as Jesus was handed over to the people (a crisscross between heaven and earth), in an effort to help us learn about sacrifice. God doesn't ask anything of us that God isn't prepared to do to help us. If we refuse to reflect any of the qualities of the divine, then that is a point where humankind is lacking in experience and wisdom and a sign to God where our life lessons need to grow.

Before Jesus was sent, sacrifices of animals were performed to symbolize the cleansing of humankind through the test of Abraham - the test of personal sacrifice for the greater good. But it was not God's desire to see anything suffer. God wants a contrite, repentant heart. It was due to man's stubborn, rebellious heart that the need for sacrifice came to be. The substitute of animals was used as a symbolic lesson for the call of humankind to sacrifice our will into a willing submission to heed God's warning. We are to purify our inner self by symbolically "burning" away the untamed animal nature. We should want to serve God by helping to bring all people to rebuke sin and turn back to live an upright life.

God is searching for people who will reflect the faith of Abraham, who will forfeit their own desires to obey the will of God for the good of all humanity. When there are people drawn to do harmful things against other people, then we must learn self control to refrain from our own alluring to do wrong. The people who dedicate their lives in the service of God dedicate their lives for the good of all humanity. They will have their sins forgiven, washed clean away, and placed upon the scapegoat when they are called back to God.

In the story of Cain and Abel, Cain murdered his brother Abel who lived a righteous life. Cain was envious of his brother because Cain focused on his own selfish ambitions. He wanted to be the best in God's eyes but did not offer his first fruits in joy to God as Abel did. Cain held back from his offering and put himself before all others. This was an example of the opposite of Abraham's test. Cain did not consider the welfare of his brother's life and brought him into harms way to serve his own ego of superiority. In ignorance, Cain figured that if he killed his competition then he could take his brother's place.

This story is also symbolic further into the future when humankind sought to kill Jesus when he was innocent of wrongdoing. Jesus, like Abel, lived a righteous life in the service of God. Like Cain, many people seek power for themselves and trample on the innocent to gain success at another person's misfortune. This lesson was told in the scriptures because killing our brother does not bring us closer to God. It does just the opposite. It is wrong to live self serving lives while harming our brothers and sisters.

Those who sought to destroy Jesus committed the same crime as Cain. The religious leaders and those in authority in the time of Jesus would not accept that their own ideas and way of life was not in line with the proper way of life that Jesus lived by example of the divine. In ignorance, they *thought* they were doing what was required of them through the scriptures. They continued to sacrifice animals and performed their rituals to stick to their traditions. But they missed the whole point of the lesson of sacrifice. They would not see that their hearts were far away from the true purpose and intent that these duties were trying to teach. (Refer to Isaiah 29:13-21.)

Jesus was sent to earth to enlighten people about the error of their ways in order to bring people to repentance so that they could find a better life in peace with one another. In the face of truth, many people rejected God's own likeness reflected in the person of Jesus, the anointed Christ. Jesus was the choicest of God's own spiritual children. He was the first fruit given on the alter of God as a living sacrifice of love. Because Jesus gave his whole self to the service of God as a living sacrifice and suffered at our hands for the will of God without rebellion, Jesus was resurrected and given eternal life in the Kingdom of God. Jesus was taken back to God's Kingdom in the heavenly realm after he suffered the burden of our sins for our sake. When people repent, our sins are removed as a discarded filthy garment and thrown out to the farthest reach away from God.[78] Our sins were removed from Christ and placed on a scapegoat. This is why two goats were used in the sin offering.[79] Jesus committed no sin and cannot be eternally punished for our transgressions. Jesus bore the pain of our injustices to try to bring us back to the ways of God. Jesus can't force us to follow the ways of God. That is our choice. After Jesus ascended to Heaven, he became a permanent member of God's Kingdom because he reflected the nature of divinity. Just as a child on earth remains genetically linked with his biological family, Jesus remains spiritually linked with God's Spirit. They become "one" in the nature of the spirit, in harmony with the divine.

But what people don't seem to understand is that this is God's plan for all of us. He wants all of us to become in spiritual likeness of the divine Son, the Christ. *"You are to do as I have done for you."*[80] God wants us to return without blemish, without wanting to sin, and to be dedicated to his service.[81] This is proof that God loves us even though we wouldn't live without sin. God gave us a way to be cleansed.[82] But our duty is to forsake the ways of sin and turn back to God. We can't continue to do wrong while ignoring the consequences of our sins. *"No athlete can win a prize unless he has kept the rules."* [83] We must pursue in defeating the ignorance of our world and overcome the temptations to commit wrongs. When we rise above this world, then we may eat from the tree of eternal life and become a permanent member of God's Kingdom, just as it was God's initial plan from the beginning.

Can't you see how urgent it is that we reject our ways of sin? We must learn to rise above the hate in this world and stop harming each other. God wants all people to be brothers and sisters in one humanity. We must restrain the impulses of violence and learn to live together in peace. Jesus' precious blood was spilt for our benefit, for the hope of humanity to return back to the ways of righteousness. If we deliberately choose to sin and rebel a life of goodness, (causing separation from God), and we continue to live solely hedonistic lives (living only for self indulgence with no regard for others), then we will have deliberately chosen to descend to destruction.[84]

Jesus poured out his blood to cover our sins with atonement.[85]

Divine Symbolism

Don't let his outpouring of love go to waste. We must rise above our transgressions and reject the temptations to do harm. That takes deliberate effort and deliberate choice to want goodness to guide our hearts over the temptation of the carnal mind.

The purifying water was changed to blood - one of the symbolic warning signs when God told Moses to touch Aaron's staff into the water and the water turned to blood. Another example was when the water was changed into wine at the wedding feast when they ran out of wine. The water was changed into wine to symbolize the joy of our salvation. We are cleansed through the sacrificial blood of Christ, not because he died, but because he poured out his love and mercy for us. He did what he did for the glory of love. It was a matter of the heart, the intent of the sacrifice.

When the angel of death sees the sanctifying blood on our door, it passes over us (this is symbolic of Passover). This door represents our future life choices. When we confess to want to live in Christ, this means that we choose to live with a more positive, loving nature, but we have to truly mean it. We must choose to follow a higher path of morality and kindness. Through a renewed heart, we are given a renewed life to make better choices.

When we choose to accept Christ into our lives, this means that we should emulate the essence of Christ (khristos) within us.[86] We should be in unison of purpose and in harmony with the will of God.[87] It's not about converting to a religion called Christianity or any other religion, but about *who* we are inside. When we don't even try to reflect the ways of goodness in our lives, then our chances of staying in the Kingdom of God in the afterlife are forsaken by our own rejection of all that is good. God doesn't reject us, but when we reject the ways of the divine nature, then we are not in harmony with it.

When our physical body dies, God places our soul where we

belong according to the value of our life energy. If we don't emulate Christ within, then our soul energy won't fit in with the Kingdom of God in the afterlife. Therefore, we will be aligned with one of the lower realms where our life energy matches. If our goal is to live in the highest realm(s) in the afterlife, then we need to reflect positive energy which is in harmony with the divine energy. We must evolve in the spirit to fit in with the highest of realms - if that is our goal. The stronger our soul's energy evolves in the ways of love, the higher our soul evolves toward the light. The stronger our soul's energy gravitates toward the negative path, the deeper our soul regresses towards destruction. Our life energy then deteriorates and becomes more corrupt the farther we stray from the divine life energy.

There are many degrees of greyness between darkness and light, between corruption and perfection. The only way to evolve upward in the spirit is to learn to evolve through life experiences. We prove the nature of our spirit each and every time we make choices. We need to realize how and why many of the choices that we make, and the actions that we do, are harmful to us and to others so that we may put an end to it. We must reject our own alluring of the lower nature through repentance. Our salvation is through our sincere remorse of our wrongdoing and by emulating the nature of Christ within. I'm not asking anyone to convert to a religion. I'm talking about emulating all of the loving qualities, which when practiced helps us to rise towards our higher self. We must learn to snuff out any feelings of hate and revenge by rejecting to do harm against others. We must make the choice to participate in making a better world by aligning ourselves with a mindset that doesn't want to do harm to others. If we can cut the crimes committed in our world in half, that would make a huge impact! This is why it was necessary to make rules and rituals. Rituals are supposed to remind us to think before we act. Unfortunately, rote rituals have in many instances become negligent of what they represent.

In Jewish tradition, they place a Mezuzah on the right side of every door post of their home. They touch the Mezuzah with their fingertips and then kiss their fingers whenever they enter or leave the house. This is done to trigger a remembrance of God and the divine guidance to live upright lives as we make choices on our journey through life. Some traditions use a small vessel of water for this purpose. The water symbolizes cleansing and purity. We must keep on trying to live a clean, moral and ethical life. This is what we should think about if and when we practice this ritual. The intent of what the ritual represents is more important than the ritual.

In the end, God will see our life energy for what it is. If our spirit is heavy with dark energy, we are held accountable for deliberately turning away from God and refusing to turn back to the light. No one can stand in our proxy in Heaven. Jesus interceded for those who repented and they received forgiveness. But those who have not sincerely regretted their wrongdoing and continue to do wrong, are responsible for their own ruin. If we continue to sin after knowledge of the truth, then our sin remains.[88]

Those who have not found salvation will have their lives laid open before the presence of the Lord and God will determine where they belong in relation to the light. If these people knew any better, they could have had a higher standing in the Light. The choices that we make in our lives determines our position. This is why we were instructed to spread the news to all nations. Everyone must be given the opportunity to hear the truth to be able to understand that we choose our own destiny by what we do here by our own free will.

If we want to rise above a world of conflict and live in a higher peaceful world, then we cannot continue on the path of destruction. We cannot continue to spread havoc and violence. There is a better way of living and all of us can experience this if we deliberately choose to rise above the sinful nature. It's going to take a lot of love to change the way things are. It's our choice. You will be utterly amazed by the transformation of our life experiences just by seeing life from a higher perspective.

Chapter Fifteen
Diversity and Traditions

So, what are some of the things we've misunderstood? From the visions that I've had, it's a jumbled up web with so many twists and turns! Let me start off with explaining that there are people in all walks of life around the world who demonstrate a virtuous, moral lifestyle. They come from all cultures, religions and ethnic backgrounds. These people are the compassionate humanitarians who embrace diversities of other people without prejudice. These people can see the importance and value in each human life and they desire to live in peace with all people. They are friendly to all people regardless of the myriad of differences. They acknowledge value in learning from other people. They recognize that there is purpose and reason for all things on our earth. We may not understand everything from one perspective so sometimes it takes an objective view from outside the box to see solutions to certain dilemmas. We must learn our lessons about life to overcome the ignorance which breeds hate and war.

Our goal is to find harmony and balance in all things in a polarized world. It takes people of vision to try to help reform bad situations and turn them around into peaceful solutions. If we want to live in a world of peace, then that peace must begin from within each of us. We must learn how to tolerate our differences and value each person for the purpose God designed in each of us and in each creation.

Our world was not filled with duplicate clones of all creatures. Some creatures are similar and some are not. There is a myriad of differences within the animal kingdom just as there are within the insect, flora and rock kingdoms. While all of life reflects the same basic laws of nature, there are also innumerable variations. Does each flower have to reflect the same color or the same smell to be classified as a flower? Do all mammals have fur and four legs? Do all humans have the same eye color, hair and skin color? No, we were all created in diversity. If God intended diversity throughout creation, then why shouldn't religion also reflect diversity while still consisting of the basic fundamental guidelines? God inspired a diversity of knowledge through infinite ways which was designed for our unique cultural needs. Yet they reflect the same core elements of truth.

Although there are certain groups of people who gather into different variations of religion, this does not necessarily mean that all people within their particular group believe in the exact same way in their heart. They have many similarities and many unique differences in how they understand even the same scripture that they study. Who can know for certain which person understands their scripture exactly as God intended? In a world of diverse levels of intellect and experiences, we come to understand what we learn through life experiences. As we mature, we see things in a new light than how we thought as a child. We come to appreciate things that we once didn't understand and we acquire an appreciation for discipline and wisdom. We develop skills and abilities which were difficult as a child. Just as we mature in our abilities and appearance, we should also mature in our spiritual perception.

As a young child, we played and fought with our peers, but we didn't come away wanting to kill off our foes when we disagreed. Some of us may have had fist fights but we should have been taught to tolerate our differences. We learned to forgive and forget our quarrels and then move on with our lives. Why do so many people grow up to hate people simply because they differ in religion, opinion or appearances? We weren't born with these attitudes. We were taught to fight against diversity. We were taught to fear and to hate people through prejudice. We were taught that certain groups of people were superior while others were inferior. We were taught to fight to be on top by defeating the weak. The "superior complex" became arrogant, controlling, and aggressive in nature while the "inferior complex" was meek and suppressed. Those who were taken advantage of became resentful, and life unfolded accordingly. The development of our ego resulted from which group of people we were associated with. Thank goodness all people weren't taught this injustice, but the human race has always needed to evolve from many scars from this state of prejudice, and it still does.

In a world of polarity, some people are tolerant of our differences while others develop intolerance of difference. At one end of the spectrum are the people who are so passive that they let wrongs go unpunished. Their way of extreme passive nature permits mischief to go rampant and undisciplined. At the other end of the extreme spectrum are those who punish every tiny infraction and they have no room for dissent of opinion or difference in appearance. They want absolute conformity in thought, appearance, and behavior. This destroys the beauty of life and takes away free will. Either extreme of polarity may lead people to fall into depravity if they don't find temperance to meet in the middle. We need to find a balance where harmful mischief is restrained as well as people aren't overly constrictive or oppressed. Sometimes dissent is good when it helps us to think and evolve.

First of all, we need to recognize the middle line where discipline develops a life of upright morals and virtues. That discipline can't be too strong because we need to understand how intolerance to any and all diversity leads to breeding contempt and revolt. All people have gone astray one time or another in their life. None of us have lived a spotless life of perfection and so no one has the right to wholly condemn another person nor a group of people for whatever their differences may be. Should we then annihilate all of the roses in the field simply because they have thorns and their colors differ? Should we destroy any of God's creatures because they aren't human? Then why should people destroy other people because they differ? Only God has the right to judge us because only God knows our individual worth and value. If God who is the giver of life judged any human unworthy of life, then shouldn't God be the one to take away that life? No human is the source of all life so we should not condemn to death any life God gave. What we should do is identify the error of man's ways so we may correct ourselves and find that balance.

It is ignorant for people to fight over religion if we haven't even truly witnessed the things of the spirit. Memorizing scripture and regurgitating it is not being a true witness of the *Living Word*. The words must come alive for us to be a witness. But if we don't understand it, then how can those scriptures guide and live in us?

When people fight about religion, they are really fighting over misconceptions about faith. If the scriptures came to life in your life, then we've lived it and there wouldn't be any misconceptions if we truly touched what they speak about. Misconceptions lead to unnecessary bigotry when in reality their minds are veiled with ignorance. In ignorance, people fight and kill over religion which disgustingly turns divine guidance upside down. Prejudice which leads us to war is a product of ignorance which is a destructive energy, while peace and tolerance is a product of understanding, a healing energy. If the things we do spreads violence, fear and death then we're heading in the wrong direction.

The word *Israel* means "he struggles with God." Actually all people struggle to understand God. God had instructed through guidance given to Moses: *"Hear, O Israel, the LORD is our God, one LORD, and you must love the LORD your God with all you heart and soul and strength. These commandments which I give you this day are to be kept in your heart; you shall repeat them to your sons, and speak of them indoors and out of doors, when you lie down and when you rise.* ***Bind them as a sign on the hand and wear them as phylactery on the forehead; write them up on the doorposts of your houses and on your gates"*** [89] This is part of the Shema that the Jews keep on pieces of parchment paper, within the Mezuzah, which is attached to the right side of the frame of their doorposts. The Shema consists of Deuteronomy 6:4-9 and 11:13-21. They also keep another commandment called the Devarim (Exodus 13:1-10 and 11-16) with the Shema. These commandments are also kept inside compartments that they attach onto their head called the tefillin, and onto their arm called the phylacteries.

In the literal external interpretation, the Jewish people have written down these commandments on parchment and literally wear phylacteries on their arm, hand and head. They have wrapped their left arm with straps because it states to "bind them as a sign on the hand". This practice became a rote ritual, but as God is spirit, these guidelines were supposed to be applied *spiritually*.

The left hand is symbolic of the lower nature which is in resistance from God. It is good to restrain our lower nature so that we learn to overcome our impulses to do wrong. (The Jewish scholars bless with the right hand and keep it slightly higher than their left arm, which is symbolic that the right hand represents the higher nature of the spirit.) While literally binding the left arm with straps, we need to be careful not to hold onto doing bondage. The literal interpretation of wrapping their left arm with straps means nothing in the spirit if people don't apply the spiritual application. God doesn't give us guidance to do something without there being a beneficial reason for doing so. We can't tilt the literal interpretation so that it overrides or rejects the inward, spiritual application.

The outward application of this covenant was to remind people to perform what God guides in the spirit. The literal outward interpretation is a shadow of the spiritual interpretation. God communicates with us through images, which is most likely how Moses received the covenant. During such visions, a *knowing* comes along with the images which communicates to us the intent of the images. To a person who does not have this knowing, they can only understand the visual images through their human perceptions. So when Moses delivered the message that he received in spirit, he shared about the images that he saw, but was he able to explain the gnosis (ie: spiritual understanding) to the people? I believe that he tried very much to do so.

When I think about the visions that I had received, some of the visions would not make sense to me unless I also received the *knowing*, or the gnosis which accompanies the images. If I were to share with you only the images without the gnosis that I received, then the message would be incomplete and confusing to understand. It makes sense to me now that when the religious leaders constructed the 613 commandments from the covenants that Moses received, that they most likely made them without understanding through the *gnosis* that I presume Moses received. I'm sure that Moses understood the covenants, but to explain them to other people into a language was difficult when their minds were cloudy of such spiritual intentions.

The spiritual intent of Deuteronomy 6:9 is to: keep a strong hold (bind) onto God's guidance as a reminder (sign), and remember them while doing service (on the hand) and constantly reflect on them in our mind and thoughts (wear them as a phylactery on the forehead). In other words, we are supposed to always keep *mindful* of God's guidance and to *do* what they guide wherever we go, whether at home or elsewhere.

While people struggle to understand God's ways, we have time and again interpreted God's guidance in the literal sense without applying the inner message which is always trying to develop our inner state of being. God was guiding the actions of our heart, not watching for literal signs (rote rituals) of this act. What good does it do the human race if we don't stay mindful of God's guidance and live by them, not by our outward display, but by the heart? I don't know if each individual Jew does the "inner work" on their heart, mind and actions, but we certainly do see them performing the rituals of the outward application. It was because of these outward applications that Jesus was admonishing them to understand the spiritual.

"The true Jew is not he who is such in externals . . . The true Jew is he who is such inwardly, and the true circumcision is of the heart, directed not by written precepts but by the spirit; such a man receives his commendation not from men but from God."[90]

In a polarized realm, the carnal body is in opposition to the spirit. As a result, when people turn only toward the outward interpretation without developing the inner application, they don't find the balance to mature in our inner being. We need to find the harmony of the literal words with the spiritual application. Otherwise, we may bring curses or calamities upon humankind if we insist on the extreme polarity of the physical, literal interpretation without yielding to the inner spiritual guidance. I'm afraid that this is what happened because as history reveals, the turmoil and wars fought in Israel continues.

Since we are still struggling to understand God's guidance, we may form human interpretations which are in opposition to God's intent. There is a difference when we interpret God's Word into the human interpretation rather than the spiritual intent, and that is why we were told to do what is right in <u>God's</u> eyes, through the divine perception. We must seek a higher conscience to understand God's Word with a spiritual perspective.

"It was there that the Lord laid down a precept and <u>rule of life</u>; there he put them to the test. He said, 'If only you will <u>obey the Lord your God</u>, if you will <u>do what is right in his eyes</u>, if you will <u>listen to his commands and keep all his statutes</u>, then I will never bring upon you any of the sufferings which I brought on the Egyptians; for I the Lord am your healer.'"[91]

When religious leaders don't understand the spiritual intent of scriptures they make laws and rituals which reflect their literal interpretations. They insist that their interpretation is right because they literally did what the scriptures said. Unfortunately, many of them missed the point for this symbolic ritual and they continue to have sufferings. They then try to justify the sufferings when it was not God's will for them to constantly suffer. This began the self-righteous attitude of the Pharisees and Sadducees who would not see what God's prophets and messengers were trying to explain. In their way of thinking, (from their mortal point of view), they were keeping the commandments by performing their traditions of rote, symbolic rituals. These rituals were fine to perform in the hope that they will come to realize the intent of the symbolic ritual. But if they did understand them in the right light, then why do they still suffer? They are still a devoted group of people dedicated to their traditions. They read God's Word, but is it possible that many of them still do not understand the point? Remember it is written: *"if you will do what is right in <u>his eyes</u> . . . I will <u>never bring upon you any of the sufferings</u> which I brought on the Egyptians"*.

They remain proud and steadfast to their written laws, yet many were lead astray by not doing what the covenant taught from the spirit. What good does it do anyone to hear the law if no one obeys the covenant of the spirit? What good does it do to recite the scriptures when we don't understand what they mean? (Muslims and Christians do this too.)

To this day, the Jewish people are still suffering persecution, and to this day they have kept their traditions alive. They have free will, and they may continue in their ways as long as they choose to do so, but something is wrong if they continue to suffer. I would like to see them set free from persecution. Is there some way in which they've overlooked some of the spiritual application of the scriptures? I know from my own experience that God searches our hearts for true worshipers in the spirit and not for just keeping outward rote traditions. I do admire their perseverance, so why do they continue to suffer persecutions?

As I reflect on this, I think about the example of apostle Paul when he was confronted by Jesus in the spirit on the road to Damascus. This was about thirty years after the crucifixion. Paul was a devout Jewish Pharisee, (previously named Saul until his conversion). He was well versed with the scriptures but savagely persecuted the Christians until he was blinded by a bright light. Jesus spiritually appeared to Saul and asked him why he was persecuting him. Saul was strongly devoted to the traditions of his ancestors' religion with so much zeal that he persecuted the church of God.[92] When the spirit of Jesus confronted him, Saul had a choice to make and he chose to transform his ways. He switched his rigorous devotion to embrace Jesus and to stop persecuting his followers. Saul's heart was changed on the inside to follow the path of the spirit.

Saul couldn't see the error of his ways before his conversion because he was blindly devout to his outward religious traditions which were in conflict with the spirit. It took the intercession of the *spirit* to help him see the error of his ways. Like Paul, all people need to try to evaluate our own lives and motives to see if we may also be blindly doing things in the passion of religious fury which are not peaceful or in line with the spirit of love. We need to learn through the mistakes of others and not make the same mistakes. We have to get back on track to be healed.

I know that any person in the world, of any race or religion, who spiritually reflects God's guidance upon their heart, thought, and actions, are seeking and fulfilling the spiritual statutes. Most religions do teach God's guidance which can bring us to peace, but the followers have rebelled the spirit without realizing what they do. God loves all of Creation, but people do not know God's way without divine help. That is why God sent prophets and messengers to try to correct their misunderstanding, but instead, God's messengers were persecuted. *"The lesson was not learnt; still your own sword devoured your prophets like a ravening lion."* [93]

God is love and spiritual guidance is about the spirit of love. We must permit people who are inspired by the spirit to voice their opinions because we don't want to be wrongly persecuting God's chosen messengers who were sent to help all of humankind to better understand the spirit of the Word. The test is the conformity of their message with love, truth, compassion, and mercy. Any person who leads people to destroy the diversity of our human race is misguided by distortions of their heart.

With each additional interpretation of God's guidance in the past, people have succeeded in confounding their understanding even further because people continued to believe in their *own* human perception instead of seeking God's perception. *"My people have forgotten me over and over again."* [94] People don't realize their mistakes until the light penetrates their heart. Humankind was permitted to continue learning through life experiences in hope that the consequences would reveal the error of their ways and guide them to find the right path. But some of us never have learned through the consequences. They did not follow the spirit of love to adhere to the proper perception of the Word.

The human interpretations from religious clerics formed rules which became so burdensome that no one could keep them. Thank goodness that God does not keep the 'no tolerance' rule, otherwise, no one would make it to Heaven! Jesus came to ease our burden to where we could understand religion in a more simplistic way by watching him live out an example of the living Word. God didn't give us guidance to burden ourselves with picky repetitive nuances and rules that didn't bring us closer to God in spirit. If you haven't experienced any spiritual things in your life, then you may need to re-evaluate your perception. Why have a religion if you don't reconnect with God? That's the point of religion!

The first commandment was to love God with all of our heart, mind, and strength, and the second commandment was like it - to love one another. Love is the core of God's will. If we study all scriptures from the various denominations of faith, you should find this same core message. If we interpreted God's Word in our hearts with a spirit of love, we would keep and honor it. Anything that we do in opposition to God's way is against the spirit of love. Those who keep to the rebellious side, will not evolve upward in the spirit. They will be bound into the slavery of this world until they let loose the fetters of the destructive, negative pull. Only God knows the hearts of men and only God can fairly judge whether a person or a nation has deliberately rebelled or honored God's way.

People who continue to hate and unjustly kill one another will keep the nature of evil and sin alive. There are consequences to pay to balance the scales of divine justice. It is one thing to defend yourself in the event of a deliberate attack, and another to tip the scale of injustice by causing murder and unwarranted violence.

An 'eye for an eye' and a 'tooth for a tooth' did not mean to do more bad for bad. We do need to discipline the wrongdoer about the wrong he had committed, but it's by teaching them the correct rules of conduct, in an effort to undo their damage. Discipline is for the correction of misbehavior because there is a consequence to balance the infraction.

Unfortunately, humankind has taken "an eye for an eye" as their right to avenge. They misunderstood the correct concept. We are supposed to restore or undo what our misbehavior did to infringe or bring harm to another. For example, repair their vision for the eye that can't see, meaning teach them what they don't understand. Replace the same amount of money that was stolen back to the victim, etc. We need to repair or undo the damage that we do to others if at all possible. If that calls for paying medical bills for harming another person, then we need to do what we can to help people to heal.

"He whom God declares to be in the wrong shall <u>restore</u> twofold to his neighbor."[95] Why twofold? In the case of a thief, one is to restore the damage done to the victim, and one is for repentance to offset or counter balance his crime. A thief took and so a thief must in turn give to balance out his infraction. Again, the intent of stealing was taking away what belongs to the rightful owner. To counterbalance this crime, the reciprocal of taking away is to give, thus the thief repays twofold. The thief's debt is paid-in-full when he gives in surplus beyond what he stole. If a loaf of bread was stolen, then he should return a loaf of bread plus give a gift for remorse for his misbehavior.

Every action that man does has an impact on others around them. The energy then in turn affects the overall universal scale of humankind, which affects the world's energy, either positively or negatively. Whichever side the scale is tilted toward determines the overall effect reflected in the world. The condition of the world results from our actions and is an indication to God and to us whether we are turned toward or away from God.

People say that they want to live in a peaceful world, but they don't know how to live in harmony with diversity. How can we understand what God wants if we continue to take everything that scripture guides from our human point of view while repelling God's spirit? Would you be willing to lay aside any hatred and thoughts of revenge to transform the world into peace? Can you imagine the huge transformation in our world if all of us would stop taking revenge and instead sought peaceful solutions? All we have to do is turn to God, toward the point of view of mercy and forgiveness. Killing a person because they killed someone else is doing wrong on both sides. It is not undoing any crime. If instead, we educated them not to take revenge, then wars would become obsolete because we would stop the bloodshed! As long as people believe they have a right to have revenge for every little infraction, then the killing will continue to go back and forth and we'll never find peace.

I need to clarify something about 'religion' since religion has been used to ignite wars. Most people want to believe that their religion is 'the only' correct religion and are afraid to embrace other concepts in other religions. It is understandable to me how people came to this conclusion according to their interpretation of scripture: *"Understand that this day I offer you the choice of a blessing and a curse. The blessing will come if you listen to the commandments of the Lord your God which I give you this day, and the curse if you do not listen to the commandments of the Lord your God but turn aside from the way that I command you this day and follow other gods whom you do not know."*[96]

People are afraid of being led astray by learning from another religion that their own religious interpretation shuns and condemns without full knowledge of what they are condemning. Again, this fear of other religions comes from misunderstanding the proper intent of scripture because people lack a universal perspective. If your religion explains that God wants all people to live in peace, then why can't people understand that forcing people against their will to conform to a particular brand of religion does not lead the whole world into peace? The human race has always fought this battle for religious domination and we still haven't found peace. How long do we continue to fight wars of religious persecution until we realize that we were wrong? Thus, we misunderstood the intent of scripture!

The Bible refers to those who follow God's ways as God's chosen children, and those who do not as rebels or foreigners. They are foreign to God because they are not like God. They are rebels when they rebel from divinity. Those who follow God's ways are conforming themselves in 'likeness' with God's character. God wants us to reflect the best of human traits which are in harmony with the divine, ie: love, honesty, gentleness, compassion, charity, mercy, forgiveness, fairness, humility, wisdom, etc.

When scripture warns us not to follow another god, it wasn't prompting bigotry of other branches of religion. Scripture informs us that there is only one God -- one universal Source of life. Why would God warn us not to follow another god if there isn't any other? Why would we need a warning about something that didn't exist? It's because this scripture was referring about not following the path that was in opposition to God's likeness. This scripture was actually warning us not to follow *people* as a god because no mortal human is perfect in their understanding of scriptures without God's help. If we follow those who aren't guided by God's Advocate, the Holy Spirit, then we won't have any insight into the divine perception. This is why scripture is confounded to people who are not taught by God. People who follow the path of hate, revenge and killing are lead to destruction. It's a clear sign to all that they are foreign to God's ways because they want to destroy and do things which extinguish life and prevent the ways of love and peace.

When each prophet of God was given divine guidance in the spirit, followers of that prophet turned the universal Faith into another faction of 'religion'. Faith in God was not supposed to become a battle of religions.

Each prophet had the true religion only that it was explained and expressed in diverse forms of the same truth. They were diverse as languages and cultures are diverse. God has always been the source of all divinely inspired religions, ever since God intervened with the first humans. People just didn't understand the precepts of their religion from God's perspective. God gave guidance to help encourage us to live a life which was peaceful toward one another. It was human error to use religion to separate and oppress others. All religions guide us to have brotherly love, respect for one another, and to live honorable lives. This is about our relationship with all people, not just with those who live in our own group or clan. If we truly seek God's way then none of us would seek to oppress or intentionally harm another human being, especially if he/she is striving to live an upright life which reflects God's divine attributes of the spirit.

If all people would come to view their religion through a universal perspective instead of as an exclusive club, then our world should see the unity of religion through diverse expressions. The oneness of all humanity is universal. It is not exclusive through bigotry and prejudice which is caused by ignorance.

Chapter Sixteen
Children of God

God calls those who conform to God's ways as God's "children". This intent to use *children* has nothing to do with physical conception. We did not become God's children through the course of nature of the flesh. This concept needed to be taught, although it is still misunderstood by many. All people have an equal opportunity to connect with God through the Spirit. "Children of God" do not come through the mortal flesh which dies, but are immortal through the Spirit.

Those who find a spiritual connection to God are *children* of God. They find a connection in "spirit" which has a life altering power and works in us to bring us to our higher self. Some people evolve into a heightened state of awareness that this world does not understand. They receive inspiration and revelations from a higher source and they come to know God the heavenly Father because they are 'in tune' with each other. This is why Jesus said that if we knew him, then we would also know 'The Father' as well.[97] This is how the two becomes one in harmony of spirit. Jesus was Jesus, and yet the Father was reflected with him. Jesus said: *"It is not I alone who judge, but I and he who sent me. In your own law it is written that the testimony of two witnesses is valid. Here am I, a witness in my own cause, and my other witness is the Father who sent me."*[98]

Jesus is the vessel who is the very image of God.[99] *"For the divine nature was his from the first; yet [Jesus] did not think to snatch at equality with God, but made himself nothing, assuming the nature of a slave.*

Bearing the human likeness, revealed in human shape, he humbled himself, and in obedience accepted even death – death on a cross. [ultimate sacrifice] *Therefore God raised him to the heights and bestowed on him the name above all names, that at the name of Jesus every knee should bow – in Heaven, on earth, and in the depths – and every tongue confess, 'Jesus Christ is Lord', to the glory of God the Father."* [100]

Jesus did not say that he **was** God the Father but that they were *'One'* in spirit; for there is only one God who created everything. Scripture testifies that Jesus was sent by the Father and does the Father's work. He is the heir of the everlasting Father, and we are also to become heirs. *"For through <u>faith</u> you are <u>all</u> sons of God in union with Christ Jesus. Baptized into union with him, you have all <u>put on Christ as a garment</u>. There is no such thing as Jew and Greek, slave and freeman, male and female; for you are all one person in Christ Jesus. But if you thus belong to Christ, you are the 'issue' of Abraham, and so heirs by promise."* [101]

So many people do not understand that the goal of Christianity is not to be *called* a Christian, but to reflect Christ's <u>likeness</u>. Anyone (in any religion) can learn to reflect the *essence* that is within Christ. Other religions also teach and guide people to reflect the positive nature. So it really doesn't matter which name of religion we follow when the same goal is reforming us into a moral, upright person that is also in likeness to Jesus. The point of Christ's message was to follow the examples that Jesus laid before us so that we too can emulate his likeness of goodness. When we choose by our own free will and effort to try to live by the positive attributes of goodness, the Holy Spirit assists us to transform ourselves into the creation in which God intended for us to be, but gave that choice to us. We were created with diversity and a free will of our own.

If we didn't have free will then we would be as robots with identical thought, actions and appearance as an ant colony. If we were all identical robots, then life would be so boring and predictable. God wanted us to be able to think on our own and have the freedom to explore life. God didn't want us to do anything against our will, but by learning the innumerable lessons from life, we are given a life with the richness, excitement and quest of exploring and discovering adventures and fullness of being! Freedom is also an essence of God. We weren't created to remain bound in captivity. Our goal is to break free from the fetters of this world to reflect the nature of Christ. *"When his training is complete, [the pupil] will reach his teacher's level."*[102]

We strive to reflect Christ's nature, but we do not become or replace Jesus. Jesus reflects God's invisible attributes, but did not *become* or replace God. *"For there is one God, and also one mediator between God and men, Christ Jesus, himself man, who sacrificed himself to win freedom for <u>all mankind</u>, so providing, at the fitting time, proof of the divine purpose."*[103]

Bear with me with a loving nature and patience for I know this statement has begun many torrent arguments throughout our history, but the scriptures give us answers. *"A pupil does not rank above his teacher, or a servant above his master. The pupil should be content to share his teacher's lot, the servant to share his master's."*[104] We are the pupils to learn to become and share the teacher's lot. Jesus is the teacher and the servant who does and shares his Master's work. Jesus was united with the One God (in unity of spirit): God did not become two, but the two are united as One in Spirit and purpose.

This idea still remains confusing to humans because we think in limited terms. God's Spirit is infinite, everlasting and fathomless. We will never understand God while we live in the ways of the flesh, so it is senseless to argue about the things of the spirit that we do not understand. We do, however, need to beware of being brainwashed or forced to follow the interpretations of scriptures that were established by men. People are fallible and may teach in error. Each of us needs to have the freedom to believe what our hearts guide us.

When we are forced to obey a human interpretation of scripture and those interpretations are in error, then how can we find the correct interpretations if we are forbidden to search for the truth? The more we spiritually evolve, the more we will be given understanding. Without the correct understanding, how will we evolve with the right goal of emulating a Christlike countenance as a model of achievement? If any religious leader chastises any human for aspiring to reflect Christ, then they do not understand what Jesus taught. Such despotic religious authorities shut the door in men's faces, then we remain bound in captivity to the lower realms instead of attaining our highest potential.

I attest that God does guide us through our hearts if we are set free to follow the truth that we find. The spiritual blessings that God shares with us does not turn us into another God or another Jesus. We only discover that we are One with God through the spirit and God is always greater. God shares blessings with us and works miracles through us. No one can defile the spirit, but you alone who allow sin to enter into your heart can defile your self.[105]

"For God knew his own before ever they were, and also ordained that they should be shaped to the likeness of his Son, that he might be the eldest among a large family of brothers; and it is these, so fore-ordained, whom he has also called."[106] So, if we are to be *like* the Son, and the Son was sent to show us how we **should** live,[107] then we are to grow up and be joined in unity of the fullness of Christ.[108] God wants us to be connected through the indwelling spirit.[109] *"[We] have access to the Father in the one spirit . . . In him the whole building is bonded together and grows into a holy temple in the Lord. In him you too are being built with all the rest into*

a spiritual dwelling for God."[110]

Nothing can ever separate us from God's love; not even death, for we are reborn and renewed by the power of the Holy Spirit through Christ. *"He saved us through the water of rebirth and the renewing power of the Holy Spirit. For he sent down the Spirit upon us plentifully through Jesus Christ our Savior, so that, justified by his grace, we might in hope become heirs to eternal life. These are words you may trust."*[111]

The children of God do not die, just as Jesus is not dead. So where is Jesus and the children of God now? Jesus has taken his seat at the right hand of the throne of Majesty in the <u>Heavens,</u> as minister in the **real** sanctuary.[112] As Jesus was raised to the heights of Heaven, we will be raised. God is God of the living!

There are so many scriptures which testify to the spiritual realm as an afterlife. Jesus talked to Elijah and Moses after they physically left the earth, and a couple disciples witnessed them.[113] Also, Jesus said: *"For all the prophets and the Law foretold things to come until John appeared, and John is the destined Elijah, if you will but accept it."*[114]

God can raise up children for Abraham through the rocks if so chosen for all things are possible with God. The concept of the 'children for Abraham' is through the *Spirit* of faith, not through the bloodline of flesh. God wants us to be like the spiritual essence of Abraham's good qualities, not the lower nature of flesh.

This was the beginning of some confusion to the people before Jesus came as a living example to clarify their error of understanding, and still there are people who do not understand. Many people thought only in terms of fleshly descendants through a human womb. They couldn't think past biological heirs to understand that God was referring to spiritual heirs. God is the searcher of men's hearts and flesh has nothing to do with it.

A child of God reflects love of purity and righteousness in the same resemblance of the spirit of God. When we are justified by God, we are chosen and God reveals to us[115] as the Creator wants us to know God. God is the one who chooses these people and we are supposed to wait for the revealing of the children of God. When they are revealed, we should not despise or revile them. We should listen, respect, and aspire to emulate their positive disposition and not react like a tin soldier with no heart, who kills for what he cannot steal.

People do not know the hearts of another human being, so how can a person judge another, let alone another nation, to be children of darkness or of light? 'Darkness' is not seeing, which is in ignorance. Light reveals, which is seen and understood. Only God knows all truth. If anyone cannot learn to break away from the destructive forces of arrogance, self-centeredness and greed, then that person is not allowing the Spirit to enter and guide him. God threw Lucifer out of Heaven because of arrogance and it's destructive force.

Look to the rock from which you were hewn.[116] Wake up! Remember who you are. I was given a revelation from God when a large white quartz rock was demolished by a bulldozer with a bush-hog at the edge of my yard. The following day, a message hit me as though a light bulb illuminated in my mind. As soon as I received the following revelation, I ran outside to the site of the quartz rock and examined it closely. Then my mind expanded the revelation. This is one of the ways God teaches through nature.[117]

We, . . . everyone, . . . all people, came from God in the very beginning; (the whole quartz rock represented this). When we came to the material state on earth, the quartz was chopped up into fragments. The many fragments were spread out and splintered into so many small fragments (different nations, religions, or groups of people), that it became complicated and almost impossible to put the rock back together as it was.

Each religion around the world became a fragment of the whole. Each nation and religion believes they are a complete rock on its own, not seeing that they are only a chip from the grander original rock.

In time, within each fragment, some religions became worn around the edges and grew some moss and lichens until it did not fit back together like a puzzle. The 'worn out places' are things people were supposed to remember through the symbolic rituals given by God through Moses. Unfortunately the real message was forgotten and morphed throughout the ages, and the moss and lichen were the greed and selfishness growing upon our churches. Jesus referred to this as the 'yeast' that puffs up with empty air; the self-important pride.

Sitting beside the shattered rock, I searched for a long time for congruous pieces, but the rock was demolished beyond any assembly. It was virtually impossible to find just three rocks which fit back together. Only pieces with a vein of burgundy color (which reveals a common ingredient in some people), helped to distinguish some rocks from the remaining hundreds of pieces. I was able to find several couples which fit back together (this also represented the marriage of a man and a woman, but two rocks do not stay together without the support of the third rock. The third rock supports the two drawn together, but without it they fall apart. This represents a marriage which is supported with God and having strength in union with the spirit. A marriage without a spiritual union with God easily falls apart.)

Each religion learns only what is handed down to each person through the generations. People believe that their own particular religion is whole because they follow the crowd which accepts knowing only a piece of the whole truth. People do not see the moss or lichen growing within their church because it was already existing at the time each new member was brought into the fold and the people accepted the interpreted package as it was presented to them. The worn away values were not learned because it was missing from the package handed down. Whether talking about one church, or one religion, or one nation, people must learn to open their hearts and minds to the truth of God's revelations.

Gather wisdom from within and see your leaders for whom they really are.[118] If greed, selfishness, arrogance, self-importance, usurped riches and abusive power, etc., exist within your religious leader, then you must scrape off the moss and lichen to fit back into place. When these errors are purged from the individual churches, then they can be brought back into realignment with God. Jesus did not always use a building to give his sermons; he spoke from the mount, or in the streets, or in a small fishing boat. He visited various homes and spoke in friendly companionship during meals. Jesus did not hoard up anything to beautify any building, or to provide for himself to have expensive clothes or anything else. He welcomed all people into the family of God. He had no prejudice or hatred toward any group of people. I don't believe he even thought about religious division. His arms were opened wide to receive any and all who wanted to belong to God. His message was universal. He is continuing to do the same today through the Heavenly sanctuary.

"Just such a high priest we have, and he has taken his seat at the right hand of the throne of Majesty in the Heavens, a ministrant in the real sanctuary, the tent pitched by the Lord and not by man . . . Now if he had been on earth, he would not even have been a priest, since there are already priests who offer the gifts which the Law prescribes, though they minister in a sanctuary which is only a copy and shadow of the Heavenly. This is implied when Moses, about to erect the tent, is instructed by God: 'See to it that you make everything according to the pattern shown you on the mountain.' But in fact the ministry which has fallen [present tense] to Jesus is as far superior to theirs as are the covenant he mediates and the promises

upon which it is legally secured." [119]

The temple was to be built among the people on Earth because God wanted to remind us of the way it is in the Heavenly realm. The church on Earth is only a shadow of the Heavenly Sanctuary. Each item is a symbol of the true reality, only we are without its knowledge because the truth was not handed down to each generation. Moses instructed his people how to build the temple by God's request, but the meaning of the symbols have been lost to the majority of people around the world. People still perform rituals, without knowing the true *spiritual* meaning because they simply accept the rituals as something that was just done. They did not understand the spiritual significance.

If money is collected to beautify your church building or property, don't get carried away with it by forcing poor people to squeeze out from their needs in guilt. Donations and tithes should be freely given from the heart by those who can give. Can any building possibly be good enough for God who created all things? Certainly not! Anything people build and decorate cannot compare to God's glory. A cathedral is a materialistic interpretation of a temple. Even the beauty of great cathedrals do not compare with the awe in God's presence. Their beauty is exquisite, but a building is not alive. Any marvel people may build with their hands will always fall short of God's glory. Divine beauty surpasses bricks and mortar.

God is not housed by a building, but is omnipotent and omnipresent. A building cannot possibly capture that sense of awe. An elaborate building is not built for God, but for the people. These sanctuaries were intended to bring people together under one roof under God, symbolic of unifying humanity. Ultimately, God wants us to make <u>ourselves</u> pure and beautiful on the inside so that we may be a living temple.

Chapter Seventeen

Let There Be Peace

Since I'm talking about focusing on what is righteous and just, and recognizing the virtues which please God, I want to say something about the nations fighting in the Middle East, (or any nations that fight one another over religion). If only the Palestinian and Jewish nations would learn to reflect on the actions that Abraham demonstrated in which God counted as righteous, I believe there can be an answer to this dilemma of war.

Abram was kind to strangers and welcomed people into his home with hospitality. He was peaceful, faithful, and obeyed God's word. He was humble, generous, and a peacemaker; even offering his nephew first choice in land even when Abram had first rights of his own inheritance. *"So Abram said to Lot, 'Let there be no quarreling between us, between my herdsmen and yours; for we are close kinsmen. The whole country is there in front of you; let us part company. If you go left, I will go right; if you go right, I will go left.'"* [12] This pleased God so much that after Abram and Lot separated, the LORD gave Abram even more land and increased his descendants to be countless and forever.

The solution that Abram took instead of killing over land disputes was the key to God's approval of him. Even though Abram had the birth right to his inheritance, he split his land and shared it with his nephew Lot to prevent quarrels. Abram's and Lot's herdsmen, livestock, and tents were so numerous that the same district of land could not support both of them but Abram valued the life of his nephew and his herdsmen more than constant quarreling.

Those fighting over land in the Middle East need to apply the same lesson from Abram and stop fighting over the same territory as their cherished possession. All people from all nations must learn to value human life and want to live in peace more than killing each other for their greed of possessions and power. For what will happen by the tugging and hoarding but the tearing apart of the people and their possession until all is left in ruin. Neither side wins because neither wants to give up their territory nor temples for the sake of peace. Which choice was more important for Abram to make according to God's approval? Was Lot and his herdsmen forced to succumb to Abram? Were they murdered or driven off Abram's land? No, Abram cared about peace and the lives of all the people. Therefore, he chose to share his inheritance of land with Lot but to separate to keep from quarrels. Abram was willing to give up part of his inheritance to keep peace. Couldn't this be the solution about the Holy Land today?

All people love the temples and the Holy Land for honoring the miracles, wonders of God and the prophets. Why would God permit the Jews, Muslims, and Christians to share the same Holy Land if it wasn't trying to teach them to come together and to share? Our goal should not be about who gets to dominate to own and control the Holy Land. We need to encourage people to live in peace and to tolerate our differences while we each grow from our individual understanding of life.

God seems to arrange Beings in a spiritual hierarchy system not of power but of righteous purity. God chooses who to reveal divine guidance to for the purpose to hand down this information to others. There are several examples in the Bible when God chooses a child among men, such as the stories of David, Joseph among his 12 brothers, and Samuel, who eventually became strong leaders.

As in the example of Samuel and Eli, God didn't necessarily

choose the rank of a person's bloodline who descended from the top religious leaders in the temple or synagogues to become the next in line. Samuel wasn't even Eli's son.

In the story of Joseph, God did not choose a person by eldest descendent or rank. Who we customarily appointed throughout history as a priority of leadership (ie: the bloodline of conquerors) wasn't God's priority, and yet God saw something in the heart of specific people for a divine purpose.

David and Joseph both endured trials as children and were faithful to wait upon God in their difficult situations. It seems that a responsible, merciful, loyal person in God's eyes was worthy of acceptance to lead others. David was merciful to Saul who wanted to kill him, and Joseph was merciful to his brothers who sold him into slavery. Neither was vengeful for the wrong done to them.

A parable about loyalty and trust that Jesus shared was about a guard. The guard asked Jesus to heal his servant but that he didn't need to go in person. The guard was confident that once a command is given, then it is done, no questions asked. Jesus was pleased with his faith.[121]

God heard the agonizing and desperate cries of the Jewish nation and chose a man named Moses to receive guidance and covenants to help them out of their bondage and suffering under the Egyptian rulers. When there seems to be no way out, God steps in to help, but we must do our share as well. These people were to learn the correct way of living an honorable life and to be faithful to hand down these instructions to all people, not to force others, but to simply inform them so that they may choose more wisely.

While Moses was with God on the top of the holy mountain, the Israelites built for themselves a golden image of a bull-calf to worship and sacrificed to it before Moses returned. They were restless and impatient to wait any longer and were faithless of the hope of Moses receiving guidance from God to deliver them, even after they witnessed many miracles and plagues on their oppressors in Egypt. There was much correction to be done in the minds of the people. They were not a perfect example of righteous-minded citizens, yet worthy of God's love, mercy and help.

Reflecting back to Cain after he murdered Abel, God instructed that Cain was not to be killed, but was banished to wander in the desert. God seems to prefer us not to retaliate with death for murder, but to use a form of discipline. The scriptures use the number 40 during renewal: Lent lasts for forty days while we give up something we feel dependent upon (like food) and are asked to live without something as a sacrifice (to focus on others instead of ourselves, by helping another in need). Lent starts with placing ashes on one's forehead to remind us that the flesh turns back into dust. God wants us to realize that we are not to live for the flesh for it is mortal. (An explanation for fasting may be found in Isaiah 58:6-14).

Noah was in the ark for forty days and nights before the rains subsided, and he remained faithful to God. Moses stayed with the Lord on top of the holy mountain for forty days and nights, not eating nor drinking. The Israelites were led in the desert for forty years (a year for each of the forty days they spent exploring the country with wanton disloyalty), while God was explaining to Moses the steps to place them back on track.[122] It seems that the Israelites thought that God chose them to receive divine guidance because they were better than the remaining human race. If all of them were better than all other men, then why was it necessary for them to receive guidance? I rather believe that this group of people was chosen to receive divine guidance simply because God's love is merciful. I also feel that these people were needed to demonstrate their actions to the world. They were a sampling of people who were representative of all humankind and they were desperate and begging for God to help them. I believe that

God took pity on their suffrage and used their endurance, and those who kept hope and faith, as an example of the message of salvation that Christ would bring and demonstrate.

When God is motivated to act on behalf of a nation, I don't believe that God was elevating their status among men. Do people not understand that wicked rulers were cast out of Heaven and flung down because of their wicked arrogance, lawlessness and belief of being better than all others, including God?[123]Then why would God elevate any nation above another nation in superiority per chance they would feel haughty and arrogant? We must be careful not to elevate ourselves over the remaining human race. Is anyone willing to be cast down from Heaven because they refuse to submit with humility? People are committing the same sin as those wicked rulers when they think everyone else is beneath them and this is why God casts down the arrogant and uplifts the humble.

When God overturns our oppressors, we don't want to become oppressors ourselves. This behavior separates us from God. This is why their errors were documented in the Old Testament. The Israelites were not perfect, and neither are any other nation nor tribe, and yet God intervened to save them from their affliction of oppression under Egyptian rule. The Israelites were not used to condemn or rive other nations against each other, but to show all people what "human nature" is like when we're not careful of what we do. If each person traded places with the Israelites back in the day, wouldn't it be possible that we would have also chosen to act in the same way as they did? How can we be sure we would do differently?

People view themselves and think how much better they are because they didn't do as another did in sin. What they do not see, is when *they* slip or fall in a similar set of circumstances. We make excuses for ourselves but then condemn others for the same weaknesses. We clearly see the faults of others while we are in denial of our own faults. Away from public view, people don't advertise their own mistakes, though they don't hold back from pointing out the sins of others. No group of people has done better than another. There are well-doers and wrongdoers among us all. We are all learning lessons of life to choose to live in either peace or rebellion.

I hold the Jewish nation in high respect that they accepted to be chosen as a microcosm of humanity to teach humankind through the evils this world has given them and yet eyes are still closed to see with the eye of reason. People who condemn other groups of people are placing themselves in danger of being paid back in retribution for their hate crimes unless they correct themselves. That is the balance of the justice scales of life. It is our choice to make; we can choose to fight against each other or to live in peace. When we have common goals, we need to come together with respect, in harmony and peace.

God chose the Jews to teach the remaining people of the world with divine guidance and covenants to help people improve themselves. Sadly, the lawmakers and the Pharisees had made rules and punishments too heavy for the people to bare,[124] counteracting its intent. They didn't reflect a merciful, forgiving God. This is why Jesus said, *"You have made God's law null and void out of respect for your tradition."*[125] Their laws were too harsh and abrasive to allow anyone any hope of salvation; which was the intent of giving the Torah.

Why give guidelines if it were not to correct ourselves, and why correct ourselves if there is no forgiveness and mercy? How would people have an opportunity for improvement and learning from their mistakes if their punishments call for death? Would a loving, merciful God want us to die just as soon as we make a bad mistake, or would it be preferable that we learn from our mistakes? How are people to know all that God aspires for us without someone to spread the news? God pointed out people's misguided interpretations by sending prophets, messengers, and servants to teach us. If we don't heed to their warnings, how will society change for the better?

Many of the Pharisees and Sadducees of that time didn't understand the full concept of the spiritual children of God for they were still young and green about the knowledge found in the spirit. It was difficult for men not to take the laws of Moses as referring to the physical reality in which we see on Earth. This was the battle of the awareness of the carnal material world in struggle against the spirit because it was difficult for people to understand scripture from the perspective of the spirit, and it still is.

The Israelites thought they were a group of *approved* people of God because God intervened to help them, when all along they were given guidance to correct themselves. God chose Moses to instruct the people to love and to conform their ways by holding fast to God. The Jews kept the guidance handed down to them from Moses, but they also kept for themselves additional oral information about their secrets of God and developed rituals to help remember them. The problem with human error is that they didn't take to heart the understanding of the covenants with the discernment of positive, loving energy. Each time a prophet came to guide and correct their human misunderstanding, they refused to listen and murdered the prophets.[126] Their temple became forsaken by God and won't be seen again until the people say blessings on the one who comes in the name of the Lord. To this day, the fighting and killing has not ended. Have they learned yet not to kill the ones God sends to help us?

All of this reminds me of the folk song, One Tin Soldier,[127] that inspired me greatly in elementary school. This song reflects the heart of men as people conquer other people to take what they possess so they can be on top! A vicious, jealous nation gets envious of another nation and so it threatens to steal the secret treasure of their success. The nation that gets attacked must fight back to defend themselves, otherwise their nation will get annihilated. And so the townspeople savagely fought over a special hidden treasure until only one tin soldier was left alive – one lone soldier with a cold heart of tin. He digs up the treasure to examine its contents being only a letter: "Peace on Earth," was all it said.

What was the battle for if in the end, all people are destroyed? In the end they find that *peace* was the treasure all along. As in this example, our cloudy destiny to get to the top was only to live in harmony amongst other nations. This is the treasure that all of humanity wants but can't find. Why can't we live together in peace? Why must one side fight to obliterate the other? If neither side threatened the lives of the other, then wouldn't we find peace? We fight over our rights and beliefs without allowing others their freedom. We try to own and monopolize religion instead of letting it be free.

The guidance given by God needs to flow freely to help all people, but not to be controlled or enforced by armies with spiritually-closed minds. Divine scripture should not become stagnant so that people stop growing. God created all people, and all things. Nothing that exists could be alive without being created by God. By our *actions*,[128] we have chosen to be either God's children of the light, or rejected it and became the children of darkness. *"The light has come into the world, but men preferred darkness to light because their deeds were evil. Bad men all hate the light and avoid it, . . . The honest man comes to the light so that it may be clearly seen that God is in all he does."*[129] *"Let us therefore throw off the deeds of darkness and put on our armour as soldiers of the light."*[130]

God loves all people and does not wish to lose anybody to darkness. God was showing mercy and forgiveness by giving people instructions and guidelines for them to learn, to follow, to master and teach.

It was inevitable that the Israelites would receive divine guidance because God had promised to be the God of all of Abraham's descendants after him, which was a blessing for <u>all the families of the earth</u>.[131] Abraham was to become a father of a host of nations <u>if he would always live in God's presence and be perfect.</u>[132]

The Bible explains that all people with the virtue of Abraham's faith are the children of Abraham whose righteousness was passed down to all who have <u>faith in God</u> who raised Jesus from the dead.[133] This is stating that first, these people possess the virtue of Abraham's faith, and second, they believe in the power of God to conquer death. God is also calling us to live in God's presence and be blameless. *"I follow the course of virtue, my path is the path of justice."*[134]

We need to take a good hard look at this lesson and apply it in our world today. Why must the Middle East be in constant turmoil and war? Will it ever end? Do they want the wars to end? Why can't each nation see that they are not any more superior than any other people? God did not want nations to kill each other continually over religion or possessions; this is idol worship, (*"greed which is nothing less than idolatry"*[135], but in their stubbornness, they are being disciplined, yet they cannot see.

Israel is the chosen nation to be an example for the rest of the world as a mirror to shine upon ourselves. Let's take a hard look at ourselves, whomever we may be, and make ourselves a nation of good will! We can't elevate ourselves at the expense of another life. We must love one another as one humanity. Don't destroy God's land with dominion and oppression by forcing possession of it. Love and respect others as you want them to do to you. You shall never be truly righteous until you give in alms of what you dearly cherish - the example of Abram's sacrifice. God is not the temple built by the hands of men, nor the territory, nor any other form of material on earth. God is not solely contained inside of anything! God lives within us and around us. God created the entire Earth and everything in it and the universe around it, visible and invisible.

Since the Holy Land is the object of rivalry, then people should stop trying to own it and offer it up to God so that no one nation should ever own or kill over it ever again. Let it be declared holy ground to all the human race and not tread upon it with the soles of your shoes or with anything of ill intent. How can this Holy Land remain holy when it continues to be desecrated with hate and war? The Holy Land is already splattered with innocent blood! So let it be the sacrificial offering to God. Let it go! Let the Holy Land be open territory. All sides must agree to stop fighting! What have all these years of fighting and killing accomplished? Had either of them obtained peace? If only they could learn as Abram had set as an example to either religion. By following Abram's example, we may bring blessings upon humanity, but will they ever do it?

Although the Bible says that the descendants of Ishmael would "live at odds with all his kinsmen," nevertheless, we are kin! God was with Ishmael and also blessed him to have descendants and to become a great nation. Abraham circumcised <u>both</u> sons to keep the everlasting covenant. God had promised that, *"[Abraham] will become a great and powerful nation, and ALL NATIONS on earth will pray to be blessed as he is blessed. I have taken care of him on purpose that he may charge his <u>sons and family after him to conform to the way of the Lord and to do what is right and just</u>;* ***thus*** *I shall fulfill all that I have promised for him."*[136] The everlasting covenant was for ALL people to conform to the way of the Lord by doing what is <u>right and just</u>! Today's descendants of Ishmael and of Isaac must learn to value life over possessions if they will ever find peace. Unless we do what is right and just by God, then our blessings are on hold. This is why suffrage continues.

Who are people to think that God wants people to kill each other?

Let There Be Peace

Is God so powerless that the help of men are needed to do this dirty work? What were all the scriptures guiding about peace and mercy if our world still suffers from hate crimes and war? Such a God who thirsts for blood is not for peace if there is no mercy or compassion for people on either side. Men who kill in the name of God don't know God, otherwise they would not have interpreted scripture into the most vile way. Only "in spirit" may we find understanding of the spirit. Actions of hate and prejudice are of the negative, dark forces. Actions of love and tolerance are of the positive, light forces.

We must grow up into people of universal love, peace, sharing, forgiveness, kindness, etc., for each other's nation. I am directing these words to all groups who fight to own what God brings us together to share as one humanity. Get over yourselves! Stop thinking that one side deserves what another does not. This is just very arrogant thinking to believe that one is better than any other nation. We are not in a competition about God. No one is perfect. Can you not see that God disciplines those who sow corruption? Peace comes to those of good will.

People were taught by God to give away their material possessions through offerings of sacrifice. What was the reason for this lesson? Why were we asked to practice fasting? A sacrifice is giving away what we cherish to help others to survive. It is giving up your own interest or wants to find peace through compassion, to help the life of others to prosper. The goal of teaching people to fast was to train our hearts to think about others.

Jesus permitted the religious leaders and Roman government to do as they pleased with him and they spat upon him and spilled his innocent blood – just as we are still doing to the Holy Land. Oh poor Jerusalem! Where is thy peace? Jesus gave up all of himself to show this rule of sacrifice, and still people stumble over it. Jesus was not only the flesh of sacrifice, but the necessary *spirit* of sacrifice. We must learn to turn our focus away from ourselves and back to God. I believe that Jesus was warning us for times like these: *"Tell them to do good and to grow rich in noble actions, to be ready to <u>give away and to share</u>, and so acquire a treasure which will form a good foundation for the future."*[137] This is the foundation that we need to build upon! This was the action that counted Abraham as righteous! Are we conforming to this statute? Are we blameless? So, according to our actions, are we to be blessed or cursed?

Part 3

Second Session of Epiphanies of Divine Revelations

Chapter Eighteen
Bridging Heaven and Earth

The following is about the second session of visions that I received after the initial spiritual words and very intense visions about creation, religion and God that I've shared in Part Two. This session really tugged at my heart with very emotional memories. This is one of the reasons why it is less painful to be veiled from the remembrance of heaven. When I remember some things that happened in heaven, I feel heartbroken and homesick to be away from what I knew. It may be even worse than mourning someone who is dear to you on earth because emotions are enhanced in heaven. Even though I will one day return and see those whom I remember in heaven, I don't know if some of them will be there or somewhere else exploring life and learning their lessons, but I am not clear on this aspect because I wasn't shown about this. But I feel sure that we will eventually meet again and our homecoming will be grand! I will try to share with you my story about reconnecting with some of my companions from heaven.

One of my memories was playing in a meadow with other children around the age of eight to twelve, but age is a hard thing to analyze in heaven because sometimes we seem to be young children, and then the next moment, we seem to be grown as young adults. It's not like earth. I think that we appear to be what we are in character and knowledge at different memories, unless I'm seeing different moments linked together . . . and yet, time is not the same as earth. As I view these moments, I am reliving them and it feels like the first time around, but it's a life that I lived before I was born on earth.

Around a half dozen boys and girls were playing happily in a meadow which reminds me of a fresh, young wheat field. The grass was lush and soft as down feathers with a beautiful refreshing green color. I can remember our giggles and running around through the field. We had no worries what-so-ever in our hearts and we felt completely comfortable and loved.

We were kicking a round ball, kind of like a soccer ball, around through the grass, trying to hide it from one another. The grass was just tall enough to conceal it. Each of us took turns trying to find it with our mind. One of them kicked the ball past me in my direction, so I ran after it. As I approached the ball, I looked up on a wall that was beyond the field and I noticed a girl sitting on top of the wall, all to herself. She looked very lonely as her head was turned down and her feet dangled off the edge. I wondered why she was just sitting there when she could have joined us in sport. I called out to her and asked if she wanted to play with us. She raised her head to look at me when suddenly another female dashed over to me from my right side. She was very protective of the girl and explained in a matter-of-fact tone, (but not in a mean way); "She wants to be alone. You need to leave her alone and not bother her."

I asked the female overseer that seemed to be her protector, "But, why is she sad?"

She replied, "She misses her friend. He is not with her now and she wants to be with him."

In my mind, I saw who she was missing and I also knew him. "But, why can't she forget about him while he is away and play with us in fun instead of being sad?" I suggested.

The protector was stern and persuaded; "You cannot interfere with her. She wants to be alone."

Then I looked again to the girl on the wall. She looked at me and said, "I'm okay. I really just want to be alone right now."

I submitted in agreement and returned to the field to play with the others.

This is the memory that came to me while I visited a woman (I'll call Tam to protect her identity) who also has prebirth memories. I wrote about this experience in my second book, *Merging with Socrates and*

Prebirth Memories. We stayed up late at night sharing our memories with another man (Roy) who also has prebirth memories and wrote a book about it. That night, Tam seemed to be speaking directly to me rather than Roy while she shared her story, but she did not tell me that I was part of her story. She just mentioned that a group of children were playing in a field while she was sitting on a wall and explained why she was sad. Then, when I awoke the following morning, the above memory came to me but what I dreamt had more detail. My story was almost identical to her memories that she shared with us that previous night.

During breakfast, we compared our memories. She agreed with what I had said and told me that she didn't want to say anything about me if I hadn't remembered it, yet she felt that I was the girl in the field that came over to her, (though she didn't mention that to me until after I had told her my recollection). She verified to me, while I had verified to her, the same event as we revealed further details to each other.

I also have a secret memory after playing in the fields that I hadn't shared in my other two books or with any person until now. This memory came to me about nine months after the memory that I shared with Tam. After our game finished, the other children went their ways and I was left alone. I started to think to myself, "What shall I do now?"

Just then, a boy walked up to visit with me. He seemed to be a couple of years older than I, and he immediately captured my attention. He was very open minded and full of imagination and joy. He seemed extraordinarily different from the others and I was thrilled to be near him as we would discuss and imagine things together. He always had a way to share his thoughts with enthusiasm.

We plopped down on the perfectly soft grass and lied down with our heads perpendicular to each other. There was something about him that made my heart leap for joy. I felt so loved by him as his enthusiasm for life bubbled into an intriguing fascination. I absolutely loved being near him because his zeal for life was contageous. It was as though our friendship perfectly fit together. I could tell that he liked to be near me as much as I did him. I can still feel this love that I have inside my heart. It's quite hard to hold back my tears when I think about this memory because I miss him. I miss our close friendship. I've never had anything like it on earth. How can I miss someone who I hadn't met on earth? The heart never forgets.

I remember that he had dark hair and eyes that twinkled with love. I've never met anyone on earth that even remotely resembled his character. His smile and energy was charismatic and I wondered why he wanted to spend this special time with me. He made me feel extra special and his zeal for life penetrated my heart. I thought so highly of him and was fascinated with his conversations as he overflowed with exuberance and was in love with life. I thought to myself, "What does he see in little 'ol me?"

Shine The Light

He asked me a question that I thought was truly fascinating, but I can't remember the question, or maybe I'm not permitted to remember this. I do remember that it sparked my interest and we talked for a long time and imagined what it would be like to live in different climates on the same planet.

He was so excited as he said something to this effect, "We can be anything we wish! We can live anywhere we choose, in the desert or where there is snow, etc."

He told me of a place where there was so much diversity of life on the same planet. Some places were covered with vegetation and rich with the beauty of plants, trees, and green fields filled with rich colors, rivers and waterfalls. Another place was the opposite and covered with dry arrid sands, yet another place was covered with ice and snow. He described the jungle, the desert, the artic and the rolling hills and valleys, flowing rivers, oceans, mountains, etc. It sounded like such a magnificent place to explore. He was so enamored by the beauty and diversity of this planet.

Then I commented, "As long as I'm living with you, I wouldn't mind if I lived in a treehouse so long as we were free to listen to the songs of the birds."

I wanted to always be near him as I felt so in love with him. That's where the memory of this ends. Although it is a very short memory, it has very strong emotional ties that I can't explain in words. I remember the powerful emotions better than the words we spoke. I wish I could relive that moment, but it is only in my heart as an imprinted memory.

Another memory about this special companion is when we were a little older in stature, as young adults. I mostly remember the love that I felt inside for him. These emotions are kept locked within my heart. I could actually feel immersed in his love and see it in his eyes when I was near him. I loved to just stare at his beautiful, dreamy eyes and read the love that poured from them. This captured my heart more than anything. I don't know how to describe this love. It's like nothing I've ever known on earth. I wish I could see his eyes now. Just his eyes alone were worth going through hell, just to look at them. I would do anything for him. We were so close and I completely trusted him.

He was involved with helping the realm of earth. I wasn't too familiar with this realm, but he liked to discuss issues and problems with me. He tried to explain some problems that people had on earth. I couldn't quite grasp why people had so much difficulty on such an exquisite planet because I hadn't experienced or witnessed it for myself. He was greatly distressed over the people fighting in wars that were about things built on ignorance.

I asked, "What are they fighting about?"

He answered, "Religion. They fight over which people are the best."

I responded with shock and felt that it was quite obvious, "Don't they know that God created all of them?"

I was shocked that people on earth were far too focused on competition. Their hearts were against each other instead of embracing everyone for who they were. There was no competition in heaven. Each of us felt completely loved, secure and safe from harm. We felt happiness for each other and wished no harm to anyone.

Although this companion was deeply concerned, he was filled with love and thrived in just wanting me to listen without involving myself. I began to want to help him with his mission, but the more I wanted to help, he began to clam up about his concerns and kept them to himself. He was very protective of me as he didn't want me to worry as he did, and he didn't want me to suffer.

I grew stronger in my determination to help him, but he turned away and became more private with the issues of his mission. We were so close while he confided in me but he hadn't realized that when he started to seclude his worries from me, we began to part.

"Well, it's too late now!" I demanded as I insisted on helping him.

He had told me too much and I was now concerned about the people on earth and wanted to help him whether I was with him or not. I couldn't just stop caring. Maybe I could still help him on my own. I couldn't stand to see him holding all the worries upon himself. He had so much love within him but he was no longer carefree in happiness while he concerned himself with the worries on earth. His love for the world overburdened his heart and I couldn't stand to see him so overwhelmed with despair.

Then, somehow, the burdens of the world were manifested onto a platter in his left hand. I felt that God was revealing to me the future of his path if he continued on with this focus. It seemed only moments ago that he was free from the weight as he shared them with me, but keeping them inside manifested them into a burden for him. Why did he have to be determined to handle them alone? He was sure that he could handle it all on his own without involving me. I felt that he had worked on this mission for a very long time. As I continued to watch him, the burdens multiplied while the platter grew and became heavier so that he held it upon his whole arm. His heart was full of compassion for the world and he chose to take the responsibility to hold up the weight of the world for as long as he could so that the world wouldn't sink down.

I looked again and the violence that people do were becoming ever increasing so that he had to use both of his arms to carry its weight. He lifted them above his head and would not put them down or the people would sink into destruction. He was torn in half with his love for me and his love for his mission. He didn't want me to leave his side and yet he refused my help. Then I saw that his determination to help them soon began to weigh him down with them. They were both sinking down together. He couldn't stand to see them die and he was willing to die with them.

But I loved him! I couldn't let him go down with them. He would be free if he would only let go. I understood why he wouldn't give up so I begged to help him by sharing the weight, but he wouldn't let me. He wanted to protect me and the world as well, and to spare me from the pain of the burden. What could I do! I couldn't watch as my heart was breaking to see him care for the world with such devotion that he would permit their weight to crush him!

"But I want to help you!" I begged in desperation again.

He would not hear of it and refused my help with love in his heart. Each time I tried to explain, again, he'd turn away and wouldn't listen to me.

"Please!" I begged yet again, but his reply was "No." He wouldn't even try to consider my help. My heart was breaking as I could see his stubbornness and that I'd never get him to listen to me. How can I help him in this situation?

Then I tried another approach. As I stood watching him, I imagined what would happen if I would take the burden upon myself as well. We'd be together and we could share the weight as I lightened his load. We could handle that weight together.

Then, I realized that he was right as I saw what would happen thereafter. The burdens would weigh less for him at the time, but eventually they would continue to multiply until both of us held a much larger weight and both of us would still be crushed! I would only delay the same inevitable outcome. Then, we'd both be in the same predicament and nothing would be better. That was not the solution to the problem. What good would it profit anyone to have the weight held upon both of our shoulders and not have the burden resolved? I had to find a way to get rid of those burdens! There had to be a way to reverse the cycle and stop them from multiplying! I couldn't stand to see him continue to lovingly support their weight and to suffer for the world while the people didn't even realize what he did for them.

I noticed that this companion reflected the sacrificial characteristic of Christ. He was willing to protect and if need be, to die for others. Jesus took the burden of sins away from those who *repented* and washed them clean. Meanwhile, the world still evolves with sin and evil from unrepentant sinners. My companion was trying to carry the burden of those who had not repented yet. He didn't want them to die and yet he couldn't stop them from sinning. Somehow we had to find a way to get them to repent so that their sins would also be removed and the load on that platter would lighten and diminish away.

If we are the "body of Christ" and we are to follow him and do as he had done, then we are to reflect Christ. [138]*"For my children you are, and I am in travail with you over again until you take the shape of Christ."* [139] Can't you see that what I've written aligns with the truth? Jesus said, *"My Father has never yet ceased his work, and I am working too."* [140] Everyone who belongs to God, strives to reflect this essence, therefore, they are all working for the kingdom of God.

Then I noticed that God the Father was sitting behind us observing our situation and discussion. He was quiet as in thought. I turned to God and discussed the dilemma with Him and said, "He won't listen to me. He won't let me help. Every time I try to help, he turns away. If I don't help him then he will sink down with the weight. I can't let him go down!"

Then I realized that the only way that I could help was if I left him to go down where the burdens began. I would have to leave Heaven and the love that I treasured to go down to the earth's realm to deal with the burdens head on. I must help the people see what they were doing wrong. I was willing to do anything to help all of them to see. I loved God and my companion with all my heart and I didn't want to leave them, and yet I wanted to help them with this mission. I wanted to see my companion back in total freedom with love that we could share again without the weight of the world. I wanted the world to evolve without their sins so that the wars would end. Of course my companion could be free if he would lay down the weight, but he *chose* to hold them to protect the people from falling all the way down from Heaven's grace and mercy. *"There is no greater love than this, that a man should lay down his life for his friends."*[141]

I tried to explain to him that I had to leave him to help free him and the world. He begged me not to leave because he loved me so much that he couldn't stand the thought of my being away from him. He pleaded as tears welled up in his eyes, "Don't leave me!"

I answered, "But I have to go! I have to make this decision alone."

Nothing else mattered to me than to free him from this burden. He couldn't understand my love for him and that I could not stand by and watch him suffer! My heart was breaking for him as I cried in agony. I now had to concentrate on my own mission, alone without him. I could feel his love inside my heart and that was the key that would draw me back to him. One day we would meet again. I would find my way back because I didn't want to be where he was not. I knew that anything inside my heart would be with me wherever I went. His love was a magnet that would pull me back. How could I fail? I had to go!

He continued to insist that I not go. I knew that I was breaking his heart by leaving, but I was desperate and there was no other way. My heart was breaking with unbearable pain. Although he didn't say this, I felt his concern for me that I would suffer pain on earth and may suffer death. He couldn't stand for me to suffer or die. Neither of us could stand for the other to suffer or to die. I knew that when my body died, then I would be free to return back to Heaven. I looked at God to receive confirmation that I would be able to return. He was hesitant to respond to allow time for me to make the choice from my own free will. Was I willing to suffer for him even if I should die? Was I willing to suffer for the people on the earth to set them free? Yes, I was committed without hesitation. I thought that as long as I could return one day, then it wouldn't matter what happened to my flesh. I'd be back and the burden would lift and the solution would be solved. I didn't care what I had to endure in pain to free him and the world. When God saw my resolve, He then nodded that I was correct and confirmed that I could return to Heaven if I made this sacrifice. God did not force anything on either of us. We both chose to help the world because we both had great compassion for the people's continual sufferage. I knew that there was no other way for me to help. If need be, I would have to give up my life for this mission, just as my companion was doing, and just as Jesus had done. I wasn't going to let him go down and I would do whatever was needed to be done to lift him up and set him free.

Someone else commented that we would forget each other on the realm of earth. I don't know who that being was, but I could sense his conviction that no one remembers. Everyone's memory of heaven is veiled on earth. He didn't know that we had a deal with God to help us find each other and bring us back together. We knew that the world would cover us with the veil of amnesia, so we made plans to find each other. As long as we both searched for God and the truth wherever we were in life, we'd find each other. As long as each of us expressed our heart to reach throughout the world in search for each other, the love within would guide us. All that we felt in our hearts would stay with us even if our memory was veiled. We agreed to always stay close to God in our lives. Within our hearts we held the key of holy love. Our love was so pure and so strong that we were sure that nothing could keep us apart forever. We had to be tested and prove that our love was stronger than death.

I took the key to my heart as it manifested on a string around my waist and placed it in the palm of his right hand. He was still crouched beneath the heavy platter held up over his head with the other arm and he still did not want me to go.

I comforted him, "I have to go. Just hold onto the key and never let go. Remember me always. As long as you hold onto it, I will return to you one day. Only _you_ have the key to my heart. I don't want to be without you, so how can I fail? That's why I have to go."

He clinched the key in his hand as I cried torrent tears while I stared into his teary filled eyes for the last time before I left him. I'll never forget the love in his eyes as they were tearing up. I had to leave quickly without turning back or I wouldn't have had the strength to leave. Oh how I hated to leave him but I had to stay strong and focus on my mission, . . . alone.

His love was the absolute hardest thing for me to leave and my heart was already feeling the pain of separation before I had even left the realm of heaven. I couldn't stand the thought of leaving heaven behind to be away from him and God. That's where I wanted to stay for eternity! And now this memory is a perpetual dagger in my heart. His eyes are still locked in my memory and I can't stand being apart. How can I deal with living on earth with this painful memory? How can I live without this love? Who would believe me if I shared this story?

Now it makes sense to me why I carried this pain within me all my life, ever since I was a young girl, and I never understood why I felt so alone and melancholy. This just gives concrete proof that God and heaven exists. How could I know and miss this deep love if I hadn't ever felt it before? How could my heart feel and remember the love that I have never felt on earth? I had to have known it to be able to remember it, otherwise, how could I miss what I've never had? Every day of my life, ever since I was given back this memory, I have felt bittersweet pain of separation from him and from God. I know that God is watching over me in this world, but the earth conceals His presence so that I cannot feel it as I did in heaven. It is very difficult to conceal my heartbreak as I continue to live each day with this rediscovered memory. This is a deep treasure that I have to bury deep within myself to suppress it in order to survive. Who will believe me in this world? No, I have to let it be known. I came to earth to testify to the truth. I have hidden my story from the world for too long. Perhaps now is the time for the world to know the truth. The truth has to be revealed to conquer ignorance. I have to expose the root of people's sins to lead them to repentance.

There is so much more to life than what we recognize. There is a higher purpose for our lives that is veiled from our remembrance. How may I help other people to realize their own higher destiny? What can I do to wake them up from their sleep? How did I break through that veil to find remembrance of my life in heaven? I wasn't given back my memory until after I chose of my own free will to give up my life in the service of God. Back in 2002, I told God with a strong conviction that I wanted Him to use my life to help this world find peace and truth. I couldn't stand the pain and agony that so many people suffer in this world. I was willing to die to serve God if that was what was needed. I just wanted to help because I couldn't stand to see people suffer. I thought, how could the suffering of my one life compare to the countless numbers of people who suffer? I had no idea where my plea to God would take me. I just followed my heart. Now I am faced with sharing my story in hopes that it will help people to understand life a little better. I must try to warn people that there is a better way of living.

Sometimes I want to remember more about my companion, but then I stop myself from contemplating further about these visions because perhaps it is better not to remember more. I don't think that my heart could handle any more memories of him. My heart feels like it's crushed as it is with the little memory that I have. I have never felt that much love in my entire life on earth than what I knew in heaven. It was a love that nothing could keep my heart from loving him. Whether with him or away, my heart would always want to be with him.

We were so close and I loved him before I came to earth. Our love was truly born in heaven. Perhaps that's why I had searched for something my whole life while the veil hid this memory and my heart had never been fulfilled. If I'd have had this tender deep love on earth before my memory of my companion was given back to me, then I couldn't say that I knew it in heaven and not on earth. My love for him wouldn't have been so strong if I had found someone else to completely replace him. This has been tied to my mission all my life! My whole earthly life had been overshadowed with a veil so that I didn't know why I had always felt so alone. Now I realize that I had already known a deep love and I was searching for it throughout my entire life.

I am grateful for the veil because the emotions in heaven are much stonger than the emotions on earth. The veil helps to conceal the pain of separation. I must try to help him even if I cannot be with him on earth. I have to try from a distance. I must persevere until my hope is fulfilled and our paths will cross. What a happy day that will be when we look into each other's eyes.

Even though I haven't met him on earth, I can feel the love inside my soul. It is only with God's help that I found out about him. Without being shown, how could I possibly search through the billions of people on earth to find him? He may be on the other side of the planet where my life would never take me. It has to be in God's control to let us meet when we are supposed to meet. This is a difficult trial and it isn't really cruel. I chose to help in this mission and there are reasons for everything. I must continue to focus on my mission. I will speak the truth to enlighten the world, even if the world may choose not to listen. I've got to try. If enough people break through their veil of amnesia like I have, and they testify to the truth of the existence of God and heaven, then ignorance will be defeated and more people will turn back to God and return home.

Then I remembered a vision that I had of this man when I was a young girl. I completely forgot about it until this vision made the past vision resurface. It gave me verification that this man was connected to me in spirit. Our missions were connected. The vision also had a powerful emotional attachment to me as a young girl that pulled at my heartstrings.

As a young girl, I had a photo of this man and as I looked into his eyes, I was drawn into spiritual visions. I believe that it was his eyes that opened the door to those visions. I wonder what would happen if I were face to face with him instead of looking at a photo! The things that I saw about this man in my visions (over thirty years ago) came true as I contemplated about his life after I discovered what became of him. How could I have seen these things decades before? The visions drew me into what seemed another world of mystery and it frightened me because I didn't understand what was going on. I remember being asked by the spirit if I would believe in what was revealed to me and if I rejected to what I saw. Somehow, God was going to use this for a great purpose should I testify to this if it should come to pass and I agreed. This was revealed to me before he married, when I was a young girl. This is why I feel so strongly that it's important for me to honor my promise to testify about my visions. Oh, but those strong emotional ties are difficult to explain.

But then, I heard some time later that he got married and so the vision as a child greatly confused me. Why was I shown this? Was it just a possible future? Does this mean that the vision of the future would be canceled? I tried to bury it in the back of my mind and live my life as if I didn't see what I did. Who would have known that this man would pop up again in my life through visions again some thirty years later! I guess our mission is still a work in progress and it needs to be completed.

It is very difficult to deal with these memories because now that I remember him, I want to talk with him face to face. I am eager to know if

God gave him remembrances as I had. It was God who brought these remembrances back to me so that I could fulfill my destiny. My life on earth is but a short span of years in comparison to eternity. I must focus on the day that I accomplish my mission so that I may go back home where I belong. The truth must be known. My life story is also connected to showing the world evidence in the existence of God and a higher realm. I am hoping that this man will come through and ride the waves with me. It is his choice whether to come forward and to testify about our spiritual connection. And yet, he has already testified to it through the work he has already done long before these visions were revealed to me in 2002. There are countless signs! But without his permission to explain, I don't know if I should share any more details about this man. I don't know what God has planned in the future for us and for the world, but I won't know unless I tell my story. How does he want it to end?

Although these remembrances are from the spirit world, I can remember only what God allows me to remember, for I am still struggling with the veil of amnesia for God's purpose of concealment. I know that this concept must be difficult for people to embrace, but it is the truth from my life experience. I also know that this concept that I shared about God is difficult to get through to people, for many still think that we cannot see

God. They don't realize that God may be seen in the spirit, and some will go to war over this. (Is that behavior within the bounds of love?) Remember what I said earlier, we cannot see God in this physical world, but in the realm of the spirit, we have freedom and it is possible to see God as He wants us to see Him (or Her). God is not ever totally known, because God is infinite and unfathomable. There is a difference between our earthly father of our physical body and our spiritual Father of our true higher self. There is an intensity of my relationship with God that is unlike any relationship on earth. All I will say is that God is glorious, loving and perfect! That is what God has shown to me. God was, still is, and shall forever be my True Father. *"I said, You shall call me Father and never cease to follow me."* [142]

I pray that my books will enlighten this world to help everyone see the truth of how the burden of sin continues to affect heaven and earth through the compassion of those who continue to try to find ways to help set us free. And yet it is not in our power, but in God's power to set us free. There are many beings who choose to help our world as they go unnoticed in this world. Many of them had made selfless sacrifices in heaven and on earth to assist God's plans.

The sins of those who have repented and turned to God have had their sins removed by Christ. I will not take for granted what my Lord has done for me. I will not just passively accept his gift of salvation without showing him how grateful I am and that I will do for him as he has done for me. I was not perfect and I needed God's grace, mercy and forgiveness. I am willing to try to follow Christ as my example. I am nothing and God's Kingdom is worth my life. That's the least I can offer. Jesus asked this question: "Will you indeed lay down your life for me?"[143] In my heart shouts a resounding yes! What we do for others we also do for Christ. I understand "the cross" of sacrifice is to lay down our life in an effort to help uplift others. That's also what my companion has done. He was trying to follow Christ's example. That is a tremendous lesson learned. If it weren't for Jesus' example of sacrifice revealed on earth and my visions, I would not have understood its purpose. Now I understand why my prebirth memories recall a guide in heaven who had asked me if I would die for love. That didn't make sense to me in heaven because death was the opposite of life.

I asked the guide, "Why would love ask this of me?" But she didn't answer me. If I didn't have Jesus as my guide to follow on earth, how would I have found my way back to God? How would any of us find our way back home when we were lost in confusion?

We must work together to stop people from wanting to harm one another, because in the end, we all suffer the pain of separation. Hate is what separates people from the love of God. The sins of those who hate all of humanity are rebelling the ways of love. The burden is growing and multiplying near the final day for them to repent so that their sins may be discarded. God and the host of angels and messengers are continually trying to help this world to overcome ignorance. We did it for the glory of love! If people are not shown their ignorance, how will they know to change? If they didn't know a better way to live, how will they see their mistakes? Heaven is a wonderful place to live, but heaven and earth are linked and affect each other. We don't just twiddle our thumbs with nothing to do in heaven. The more rebellion on earth, the more need of messengers and workers in the field. That is why God is searching for more harvesters. "For the harvest is ripe but the workers are few." I believe love is more powerful than death. I give myself in love to help this world see their mistakes so that they may turn around and mend their ways. We must pass the flame of love to enlighten the world. I hope "my little light of mine" was enough to light other candles.

    I have tried with the best of my ability to share my life openly in regards to the revelations that I had received. I never had any intention to harm any person or group of people. Any reference to the errors of humankind were told in the spirit of truth from my heart to help people see their mistakes so that they could combat their ignorance. We need to be able to understand what the scriptures truly mean through God's perspective, and not through assumed precepts of men. All my hopes are to help every race and every religion to turn back to the remembrance of God.

Once I had seen the true reality of heaven, the ways of this world have no hold on me. There is no comparison to the love, peace and bliss of the heavenly realm and that is where I want to be. I had repeatedly asked God to reveal to me any inconsistencies or misrepresentation that I may have inadvertently written, but I had only been shown support and confirmation. I pray that this God-inspired work will open people's eyes and influence them to focus on God instead of their desire to live their life on earth solely for self pleasures, power and greed. If you continue to choose to live hedonistic or violent-filled lives, your fate will lead you to where you truly don't want to go. This is your opportunity to change. When we choose to be conscious of others and we wish good will to all people, then our world will be blessed in peace, a holy world living together as one.

Chapter Nineteen
Clear Signs

I was amazed with the insights that I had received from the Holy Spirit. Since the spirit showed me the oneness of religion, I then wondered about the people who flew two airplanes into the Twin Towers in New York City. They also flew a plane into the Pentagon and another plane was diverted as it crashed into a field in Pennsylvania. These people claimed to have done this in the name of Islam. It was clear in my mind that doing such deeds was not for God's, or Allah's cause. Something was terribly amiss in the minds of those people. I wondered how could anyone interpret their scripture into such the complete opposite of God's guidance.

Since the Holy Spirit was upon me and opening my eyes to see the human misunderstandings about religion, I wanted to read their scripture to find out what the Holy Spirit would reveal to me about Islam. I purchased a copy of the Koran and as I began to read, lo and behold, the scriptures were very clear to me. As I read, scripture would stand out in my mind from the Qu'ran as well as from the Bible and I saw verification about issues that people argue about today. Once in awhile there were scriptures that didn't seem to match what I was previously shown about God and so each time that happened, I stayed mindful of keeping my heart in check with what the spirit revealed to me. I instinctively knew that I needed to read it with love in my heart and with an open mind without bias. This guidance was given "for the righteous" and I had to remain in that state of mind for the Spirit to reveal its perspective. I knew that the righteous were the people who lived in compassionate ways of love. People cannot understand the ways of God when love is not present within their being. If people read scripture with a rebellious heart, then the message would be tainted and distorted according to the biased hearts of the reader. It is essential that we prepare our hearts with love before we read Holy Words. I asked God to help me understand the intent of the scripture through God's eyes. Any message given by God would be founded upon love. And indeed, my mind's eye was opened again and I saw through the perspective of Archangel Gabriel who delivered the Qu'ran to Muhammad. This is the very same Gabriel who came to Zechariah to announce that his wife Elizabeth would give birth to a son, John, as well as announced to Mary that she would bear Jesus. John and Jesus were both endowed with the Holy Spirit, sent from God to teach the world the ways of righteousness. They did not come to be worshipped, but pointed people to worship only God and to follow the path of righteousness.

As I read the Koran, I could feel Archangel Gabriel's frustration as he delivered this Guide to Muhammad because people in general don't understand the whole message as was intended by God. Each time a messenger comes to explain, some people understand some things while other things are not. Gabriel was very authoritative, stern and somewhat aggitated that people need so much repetition of guidance but then they continue to distort it according to their bias. Even Muhammad needed words repeated due to his astonishment of being in Gabriel's presence. Just the sight of Archangel Gabriel overwhelmed Muhammad with shock and awe. I felt that this Recitation would be the final attempt that Gabriel almost did not deliver, but then reconsidered and gave humankind his last attempt to try to clear the path and steer people back on track, by guiding the people where they differed in understanding. (I noted that this did not mean that God wouldn't send someone else. This was only Gabriel's last attempt.)

So much scripture was emphasized to me about the way Islam was *meant to be* but it did not show me how Muslims understand it. (I refer to the actual guidance given through Archangel Gabriel as the Qu'ran and the guidance that was printed in book form as the Koran.) I had no problem with its guidance and if people understood it as I was shown through the spirit, then no one should even think to do acts of violence to destroy the human race. No one has a right to destroy humanity. That's insane! God calls all people to live in peace, respect diversity and do all we can to help heal our world.

Clearly, without a doubt, those people who spread havoc, violence and destruction in the name of Allah are apostates of God, yet their eyes are blinded by the darkness within them. What could be done to help them to see? They are trying to force people to conform to their understanding of Islam and yet the very act of forcing religion is against the guidance that Archangel Gabriel delivered! Someone needs to show them and teach them the guidance through the eyes of God. But who could do this? I was quite sure that those people wouldn't ever read or pay any attention to what I've shared, especially when their minds were twisted backwards and filled with hatred. They wanted to force their human interpretations onto the world even when it would never lead to peace. They were only concerned about being in charge with power and might and to wipe out everyone else who chooses differently -- a clear sign of their arrogance and ignorance. I was shown by the spirit that their actions would only spread death and destruction to the whole human race. Even between two people there are disagreements. Would the last standing warrior destroy the one and only survivor on earth who voices a disagreement? If so, then their wish is to annihilate even the entire human race (which is the intent of the warning; "If God's Abode of the Hereafter is for yourselves alone, to the exclusion of all others, then wish for death if your claim be true!"[94] How in the world could they even think that their violence and terror on humanity would lead the world into peace! There was so much distortion in their belief system yet they were so determined and brainwashed to protect it until death. And that was precisely where they were heading!

I could clearly see that those violent people were lead completely opposite of God's guidance. Their path was not aligned with the love that God has for all people. God gives guidance not to destroy humankind, but to guide us toward the ways of peace, to learn to respect diversity. It is clearly evident that God created all things in diversity. Look at all of the diversity of flowers, plants, trees, animals, rocks, and people. They all vary with color, form, size, shape, and texture -- each beautiful in their own way.

Then, about a month after I read the Koran, my husband mentioned a man that he just watched on an early television program while I was still in bed. It was near the end of the program, but I immediately perked up because the man he mentioned was the man in my second session of visions! I had no idea what happened to him on earth or where he lived, and now this information was dropped onto my lap. I discovered that he was a Muslim. Oh my God! Oh how miraculous God's plan was to bring all of these visions to me and to teach me about what Islam was *supposed* to be and a way that I could help him.

Immediately, I remembered my mission, that I needed to get to the source of where the people went astray. The weight was still building and building with ever-increasing violence in our world and my companion needed my help! How could I contact him? I got on the internet and searched for him. I found a way to possibly contact him through a forum. I trusted the Holy Spirit and did all that I could to share with him what I was shown through visions. As the years progressed, I could see a change in him and I saw evidence that he was reading my messages, although he never wrote back to me that I know of. If he did try, I didn't know that it was him. I sent him long letters via his contacts, but I was wary not to share too much if he didn't want to read it. I needed to send him little by little to watch how he reacted. I was mindful that I was not supposed to force anything on him. He had to use his free will. I asked him again and again if he wanted me to continue, but he never directly responded back. I received mixed messages by observing his actions in public displays, but mostly he seemed very mysteriously open and besides, I kept receiving encouragement from visions to continue. I felt intensely eager to proclaim what had been revealed to me from God. I had to convey God's message to help him with his life's mission.

I was in a delimma because I couldn't tell if he remembered me from heaven, and yet there were signs that he did, but perhaps subconsciously. Were his signs deliberate or just happened by chance? I asked if I may speak with him directly or if I could have verification to be sure that my messages were reaching him, but I never had concrete confirmation. I also remembered through the visions that he did not want my help because he thought that he could handle the burden all to himself. But God revealed to me that the burden was much too heavy for him to handle on his own. Here was a way for me to help lighten the load if I could share the revelations that I received from God. Would he believe me? I had to try. But unless his eyes were open, he may not believe me. Was he brainwashed by human teachings? Some of the things that he said showed some confusion while other things were fine. He seemed to be sitting on a fence, caught between two opposing views. He was trying so hard to follow God and yet was fenced-in by human teachings and he wasn't sure which teaching was correct. So I pondered about this.

The vision that I received about him revealed that he could be dragged down with them. Am I too late? But I tried to contact him just as soon as I found out what had happened to him. It can't be too late or I wouldn't have been shown these visions. I know that scripture, including what is written in the Koran, states that *"No soul shall bear another's burden. If a laden soul (unrepentant soul) cries out for help, not even a near relation shall share its burden."*[145] But it also states that *"None can intercede for them save him who knows the truth and testifies to it."*[146] And yet this man has chosen to carry the burden of others upon his shoulders to keep them from falling, even though he was not responsible for their sins. He was trying to give them time to evolve from the consequences of their misdeeds so they may turn back to the Light and mend their ways. Again, the key was for us to testify to the truth so that the people could transform their perception with new vision.

I continued to try my best to share with him, but he didn't give me a way to communicate with him in private. I was resorted to sharing some things over the open forum, hoping that he would find and read what I shared with interest, but when I did, I was viciously attacked by other forum members. Most of them would not give me a chance and if anyone had, then those people were targeted by their aggression. They wouldn't let anyone help me. They had already made up their minds about me as being their enemy without knowing me or what God had done to try to help our world to mend our ways.

This is another book's worth to try to explain all that I did and experienced by trying to shine the light to people whose minds were closed and already filled to the brim with their own human understandings. They did not know me and they constantly twisted my words and tried to snuff out anything that I shared, not realizing that it was for their benefit! I saw and experienced the depth of their ignorance and the difficulty in trying to shine the light into the darkness. After all, it is their choice to choose to stay in darkness, but if they knew what I knew, surely they wouldn't have chosen to fall all the way down to destruction. They didn't know where they were headed. I felt pity for them that they didn't know what they were doing. They were fighting against someone who was sent by God to help lighten the load, a divine plan. My companion was sent as well, but he seemed to be restrained by the teachings of human dogma. There were varying schools of thought about Islam and he tried his best to navigate the middle path. There was no way to satisfy all of the varying schools of thought because many of their beliefs contradicted the other.

How could I continue to shine the light when they kept blowing out the candle! I was as a lone candle but the flame that I was given didn't reach their wick. They were without light. I don't know how much time they have left, but the sooner they listen, the sooner the weight of their sins would be lifted. They cannot continue in their ignorance or this world will become as bad as the days when men were always wicked. God promised not to flood the entire earth again, but I'm sure that God will need to do something to cleanse the world of wickedness because they've ruined this world. If we want to avoid what God may need to do to cleanse our world, the only chance we have is to mend our own ways. But how much time do we have left? Has anyone else chosen to hold up that platter to delay the day they all fall down?

I continued onward for years although I just wanted to give up on them because I was getting nowhere. But God continued to send me visions to encourage me to continue trying to share and that this man was open and listening to me, even if everyone else was not. My companion from heaven continued to send tons of "signs" which helped to comfort me, especially when his signs were related to what I had written to him, and yet his signs were not concrete. Was he still trying to protect me? My emotions toggled from feeling joyfully elated that he seemed to understand, to confusion because some of his signs could be taken different ways. Without hearing from him directly, how could I know for sure?

Over and over again, I struggled to shine the light through the forum, but it just was not penetrating their minds. And so, I eventually chose to leave the forum because no matter what I said, they fought against me tooth and nail. Their minds were as hard as rocks. They had no ears to hear and no eyes to see. Even so, I continued to receive visions for years about this man which encouraged me to have hope. I have hope that one day, he will respond and the message will be heard, somehow, some way. I have to wait until the flame catches hold of his wick so that he may accomplish what he came here to do. Then he will be set free, in heaven and on earth! This was my mission and I have done all that I knew to do. I have kept my promise to him and to God. I have come forward and testified about God and the visions I received. If my companion truly believes in God's revelations, then surely he should believe and be supportive of me. I have more information to deliver to him, but without a way to share directly with him (wick to wick), then what else could be done? I waited to see what would happen next. In the years after, more signs came forth yet I never was directly contacted by him.

Clear Signs

And so, on December 27th, 2016, I was shown a vision that I wouldn't need to directly contact this man if I explained why Archangel Gabriel delivered the Qu'ran to Muhammad. I must convey what needs to be said, either with him or without his help. Thus, this chapter (and really all of my books) are my attempt to explain to all people what I learned from the Holy Spirit. Since I had discovered (from 9/11/2001 until today) how so many Muslims had misinterpreted the Qu'ran (in comparison to what was revealed to me through the spirit), I could immediately recognize where they twisted its guidance to suit *their* biased understanding without realizing what they've done. I know that this is incredibly difficult for them to read, but it has to be stated to give them clear warning. Religion became a tangled web of knots that's virtually impossible to untangle. As long as they held onto their contradictions to Gabriel's message, they would never find peace. I could write another book to attempt to explain their misunderstandings, but somehow I don't think that will work because so many people are set in their ways. They would most likely make excuses as they've always done to remain as they have been, even though the world has reflected back to them the consequences of their misdeeds of a war-torn world. They are the immovable boulders which block enlightenment. Besides, all that I would explain is what has already been written in scripture. It's already been said! Instead, I will share a taste of a condensed version of what I was shown in spirit, to reveal what Islam was *supposed* to guide from Gabriel's perspective.

Islam was supposed to guide humankind to live a life by the "way of peace and conforming to God's way." They were instructed to have tolerance for all people in all the variations of existing religions. They were told that there is to be no compulsion in religion. Religion is of the heart. The ways of God cannot be forced upon people because love does not force itself onto others. An act of force is aggression and a violation against our free will. Muslims confess that Islam was the true faith from the very beginning and yet I don't think that they understand what this means in the right way, for they recite one thing but do another. Islam is a shard of the true Faith, but they don't recognize that the previous scriptures of other religions are *also* a shard from the true Faith from the very beginning. They were instructed to study <u>all</u> of God's revelations and not to deviate from the true Faith. But it seems that most of them do <u>not</u> study all of God's revelations. As I observed their actions in the world, in particular the violent ones, I saw such a drastic contrast from what Archangel Gabriel guided from what the followers of Islam do. Do any of them actually follow the spirit of the Qu'ran as I had been shown in the spirit? If any of them do, then where are they?

All people were supposed to embrace all divinely inspired scriptures, regardless of which prophet gave it. *"I believe in all the scriptures that God has revealed...<u>God is our Lord and your Lord</u>. We have* *our own works and you have yours; let there be no argument between us. God will bring us all together, for to him we shall return."* [147] Also refer to surahs: *"Observe the Faith and do not divide yourselves into factions."* [148] and *"Do not divide your religion into sects, each exulting in its own doctrines."* [149]

When Muhammad received the Qu'ran from Archangel Gabriel, it wasn't guiding anyone to start another branch of religion. The tree is already full of branches! How many branches does a tree need? Too many branches will topple a tree in the wind if its roots are not strong. The True Faith already existed before the Qu'ran was given! The Qu'ran was given as an additional <u>guide</u> to encourage people to reflect on all of God's <u>revelations</u> because people were fighting against one another instead of embracing each shard of the true Faith. They weren't growing in spirit because they were stuck on themselves as being superior. Most Muslims mistakenly did what everyone else in all previous branches of religion had done. They chose to embrace only their own guidance as received through *their* prophet and disregarded all other guidance which was given to the other prophets. Instead, they placed Muhammad higher than the other prophets and suppressed or tried to cut off other branches, even though the Qu'ran guides them to equally respect all prophets. They exulted *Islam* as a superior religion (not understanding what *Islam* meant in the spirit), and forcefully tried to revert people to follow their own human interpretations through violence, making religion an oppressive nightmare again! And again, human interpretation of religion was the instigator of bigotry, a seed from ignorance which continues today.

It wasn't until after the entire Recitation was given that Muhammad interpreted the word Islam to be a new religious sect for his own people. Archangel Gabriel was shocked to hear it from his mouth after Gabriel clearly explained not to divide the Faith and not to exult in their own doctrines. I saw Gabriel in the vision re-examine the Qu'ran that spiritually manifested what he had just finished given to Muhammad to be absolutely sure that it clearly stated the true intent. Gabriel saw that all that was needed was said more than once. What was the point to continue to repeat what was already said yet again? Gabriel's directive was not to force people to understand the Recitation. He was only to *deliver* it and then it was the individual responsibility and duty for each person to come to understand it for theirself. Gabriel agreed as he nodded; "Yes, leave men (including Muslims) in their errors until the appointed time. Let men taste the fruit of their own works!" And so, Islam, like the religions before, became as it is today, with some things understood and other things not. Such is the delimma in trying to guide the human race with divine guidance when their minds are cloudy with human bias and prejudice.

It's time again, at least once more, to show all nations and all religions that they are <u>all</u> connected to God. We need to focus on the <u>root</u> source of all revelations - the One God - which inspired many people from all nations to become prophets, apostles, messengers and teachers of the Faith in God. God created the world in diversity. Religion is the same. The root of a tree is where it gets its nourishment and not its branches. <u>God is the root</u>, the source of all of our religions and we mustn't ever let go of <u>God</u>, or Allah, or whatever name you use. God wants people to focus on <u>God</u> and have nothing to come between us, not even our individualized factions and sects of religion, or variation of languages. I write in English because I do not speak Aramaic, but the intent of the message is for all people. Surely you can understand.

Each branch of religion is a branch from the same tree, only each branch divided away from the Source when we viewed other branches of religion as coming from separate gods. But if we confess to believe in only one God, then there is only one God who inspired all prophets. There are no other gods who developed their own religion. We are all ONE. We may

Shine The Light

have our own interpretations of God's guidance, but the *Source* of divine revelation is One.

It doesn't matter which *style* of religion anyone chooses as long as we truly seek God in truth and in spirit. There are those whose personalities are bold and energetic and those who are quiet and meek, thus God delivers guidance to suit our diversity. People are at different levels of understanding, thus religion varies like flowers growing from the same garden. As long as we worship <u>God</u> without discriminating among the different branches, then we are of the same Faith and united in purpose. God is One universal source of life. True Faith is believing in <u>God</u>, desiring God's presence and guidance, and following divine revelation which helps us understand from God's perspective.

*"Your community is but one community, and I am your only Lord: therefore fear me. Yet men have divided themselves into factions, each rejoicing in its own doctrines. Leave them in their error **till a time appointed**."*[150]

My spiritual eyes were opened to see the error of humankind's interpretations when we fight for superiority. This is just as Cain did when he slew his brother Abel because he wanted to remove the competition. We are not supposed to compete against each other! All of us can worship God in our own heart. God wants all of us to do our best to live a moral and upright life. We were not called to uphold any particular branch of religion above another.

I grew up as a Christian, but through divine revelations, I came to understand why people fight against other religions. It's all caused by misunderstanding God's guidance and enforcing by force the errant teachings by eliminating the correct teachings. I think that people from each of the branches have done this. Human interpretations have caused men time and time again to misuse religion as a way to segregate one from another and we developed religious pride, bigotry, and intolerance of religious diversity. This negative energy lead us into having arrogant and misguided interpretations of our religion and we developed the evils of hatred and killed one another. We did not follow in the ways of peace! It is a clear sign that the world reaped the opposite of peace because our world continues to be riddled with violence - especially in relation to human indoctrination of dogma. I don't want to partake with Cain's sin of wishing harm to my brothers and sisters of humanity. If we want a world which lives in peace, then we must embrace all people as one humanity, and as fellow brothers and sisters under God.

"Corruption has become rife on land and sea in consequence of mankind's misdeeds. [He has ordained it thus] so that they may taste the fruit of their own works and mend their ways." [151]

Because of my revelations, I embrace all religions and reflect on what they <u>all</u> say, but that's not what any Christian minister teaches as far as

Shine The Light

I know. They try to convert people to their branch of religion just as Muslims do, and just as other branches do. Each of them have been doing the same thing for generations. Now that I realize the vastness of information God emanates through divine revelations, I can understand how each religion is reflecting their own cup of divine guidance from the same ocean but they can't see the ocean! Or as they say, "they can't see the forest for the trees!" You have to rise above them to have a higher view. It is important to focus on God in spirit instead of following the precepts of men. It doesn't matter which religions people use to focus on God because it is what is in our <u>heart</u> which makes the difference between a world of peace or a world of conflict.

The Koran instructs men to *"observe the Torah and the Gospel and what has been revealed to them from their Lord."* [152] (The Torah is the divine guidance given through Moses, and the Gospel is the Good News given through Jesus.) If Muslims read and study the Torah and the Gospel as the Koran instructs, then they should not uphold Muhammad higher than Jesus or above any of God's other chosen messengers. Muhammad is not to be placed upon a pedestal or glorified, because he is only human. We are instructed to worship *only* God. The Koran points out, *"Muhammad is no more than an apostle."* [153] He is not God.

Forgive me if I sound abrasive, but I am truly not trying to insult the followers of this branch of faith, but trying to bring to light the errors of human interpretation which divided us from the ways of peace. I don't share these insights to condemn people, but to shine the light as I was shown to help people get back on track. We must be careful not to fall prey to the same sins as others had before us. Think for yourselves and stop following the crowd that is leading you to your death! We must learn from past mistakes and mend our ways. We cannot make Muhammad or any prophet an idol to worship. They were not chosen by God to be worshiped. Our goal is to focus on God wherever we are and to follow the Spirit of God instead of our selfish ambitions. The Koran contains beautiful insights into God's wisdom and yet too many cannot see. They recite from memorization yet so many confess that they don't understand what it means. Why would God deliver guidance to humankind if we were not supposed to evolve in our understanding? As the Koran says, *"Feed on every kind of fruit, and follow the trodden paths of your Lord. From its belly comes forth a syrup of different hues, a cure for men. Surely in this there is a sign for those who would take thought."* [154] I can clearly see that the Koran is guiding us to study every shard of religion (the syrup of different hues), to seek the path of God in each of them. This verse (surah) is a cure for religious bigotry. Just as the honey bees feed on the pollen from flower to flower to process honey, so should we feed on God's guidance from all religions to process the cure for our ignorance.

Every religion has its errors begun by human perceptions and misinterpretations. Islam is no different. All religions reflect spiritual truth, but it is not understood by humankind without the connection with God in the spirit. God is eternal and unfathomable, and so how could humankind come to understand the vastness of God's knowledge as if it could be contained inside of just one book? *"If all the trees of the earth were pens, and the sea, replenished by seven more seas, were ink, the words of God could not be finished still."* [155]

Divine revelations must continue if we are to learn to understand God's guidance. God never stops revealing the truth. If so, then the world would stop evolving and be engulfed in our sins without a chance for enlightenment because God does not guide the evildoers. The intent of giving the Qu'ran to the people was not to abolish God's former guidance, but to give a clear <u>warning</u> to seek God and the ever unfolding truth, in love and peace. You must read all scripture with a heart of love. The warnings in scripture may sound harsh in our eyes, but it depends on the condition of our heart. Likewise, to say that God cannot send any more messengers is stifling the mouth of God and depriving ourselves of God's assistance. Without God's guidance through revelations, humankind will only continue to plummet toward destruction through our ignorance. Our sins will continue to grow because we don't know any better. The Koran instructs believers to help those who receive revelations, and yet they interpret the tenets backwards to be the demise of revelations. How are they to help those who receive revelations if they mock and try to silence them? The harm is to themselves if they only knew it. Religion which is practiced without the spirit is an empty faith. Muhammad was an "authentic prophet", as a king uses his "seal" on a letter to authenticate that the message came from him. The seal did not mean that the letter was meant to remain closed. Why send a message if the receiver is not permitted to open the seal? If you have eyes to see, then SEE! All religions must be open to the Spirit of God for us to evolve in understanding Divine guidance.

What is so beautiful about any one religion that you cannot get from another religion? It was the *style* of the religion that you sought within that has attracted your heart. But, because other people are attracted to other styles of religion, doesn't make their religion wrong. The important factor is what placed the love for God into your heart. The differences of religion is a variation of *style* in worshiping God, our Source of life. This style comes from the traditions and customs through human interpretations of God's Word but the core message is still the same if we have eyes to see. We are to seek God and the ways of goodness and kindness, and treat all people with value and respect. We must allow people the right to openly shine the light. We should not oppress or persecute people for their faith in God simply because they use a different style of religion, or another style of language. We don't have to agree with everyone's opinions, but we must respect their right to express it. It could be a matter of life or death! Let the truth be heard and stop trying to snuff out the light. Preventing the truth to be heard only hurts the survival of the human race. Why would you want to destroy God's diversity of human life? Why would an all-powerful God use jihad to kill the people that *humans* judge as unworthy of life? Who are you to judge!

Hasn't God chosen people from around the world to help humankind? Can you see in your heart and mind the similarities of: Gandhi, Confucius, Muhammad, St. Patrick, Saint Francis of Assisi, Mother Theresa, Abraham, Noah, Moses, and Jesus? If you don't know what all of these people stood for or have an aversion to them, then you have some research to do. There are many, many more people as these in all of the major religions. Look for them all around you. *"The apostles [God] sent before you were but men whom we inspired with revelations and with scriptures."*[156] God's apostles and messengers are still around, if we can only develop eyes to see. They are still trying to help the world grow in peace. None of them came to pivot religion against religion nor to incite people to hate other people with animosity and contempt. They came with the same core message to try to unify all people into harmony and peace. They don't have to carry a title of degree from men because they have the Lord's authority. If your heart is seeking peace, then you should be able to find them by their message of peace. They do NOT rally anyone to go to war. May our eyes see more clearly and our actions be motivated with the love of God. Let's all get onboard, back on track.

One more thing. I thought that this book was finished and ready to be published, but I received another vision on the early morning of January 11, 2017 to add. I will end with the message that I understood from the vision:

"We have fallen and gotten hurt without understanding how it happened because we all think as children. Our foundation wasn't secure. It was flimsy as cardboard. We must stop the constant flow of bloodshed to be grafted back and become healed."

Shine The Light

Notes

Chapter 1: Streams of Living Water
[1] John 7:38-39
[2] Hebrews 10:16 and Jeremiah 31:33
[3] 1 Corinthians 3:8-9
[4] 1 Corinthians 4:15
[5] John 16:12
[6] John 21:25
[7] Acts 3:19-22
[8] Ephesians 1:17-23

Chapter 2: Divine Visions
[9] 1 Corinthians 14:37
[10] ref. 1 Thessalonians 5:19-22
[11] John 17:21-23

Chapter 3: My Call to Witness
[12] Acts 18:9-10
[13] 2 Corinthians 3:1-6
[14] Ephesians 4:18-19
[15] Hebrews 6:18-20

Chapter 4: The Beginning
[16] Genesis 1:26

Chapter 6: Creation

[17] Romans 1:19-20

Chapter 7: The Living Mirror

[18] 1 Corinthians 13:12
[19] Genesis 1:6
[20] 2 Corinthians 3:15-18
[21] John 14:11
[22] John 17:23
[23] Genesis 1:27
[24] Colossians 1:15-17 and 2 Corinthians 5:19
[25] Galatians 4:19-20 and Romans 8:29

Chapter 8: The Mystery of Christ Revealed

[26] 1 Corinthians 11:7
[27] Genesis 1:27
[28] 2 Corinthians 3:16-18
[29] 1 Corinthians 11:12
[30] Romans 15:4
[31] Ecclesiastes 12:12
[32] John 17:21-25
[33] Isaiah 53:12
[34] Colossians 1:17-18
[35] Colossians 1:25
[36] Hebrews 10:26
[37] Romans 2:5-8
[38] John 3:16

Chapter 9: Finding Unity with Divinity

Notes

[39] John 8:35
[40] Deuteronomy 6:4-9 and Isaiah 43:10-13
[41] Philippians 2:6-8
[42] Isaiah 43:10
[43] Matthew 12:25
[44] John 8:28
[45] John 8:50
[46] Galatians 4:19-20
[47] 2 Corinthians 3:18
[48] Romans 8:29
[49] 2 Corinthians 6:18
[50] Colossians 1:15-19
[51] Hebrews 2:12 & 17 and John 20:17
[52] Romans 15:5-6

Chapter 10: The Bridge

[53] 1 John 4:18

Chapter 11: A God of Wrath and Vengeance...My Thoughts

[54] John 3: 19-21
[55] Matthew 23:23
[56] Matthew 15:9
[57] Galatians 3:11
[58] Galatians 3:1-25

Chapter 12: Sin and Free Will

[59] Genesis 2:9
[60] 2 Peter 1:21
[61] 1 Corinthians 15:49-55

[62] 1 Corinthians 15:38
[63] Matthew 24:33
[64] John 15:27
[65] Jeremiah 18:4-7
[66] Matthew 22:33
[67] John 13:15
[68] ref Titus 3:6-7

Chapter 13: A Universal Religion

[69] Hebrews 5:12-14
[70] Exodus 33:18-23
[71] Exodus 31:18 & 32:15-17
[72] Exodus 34:1 & 27-28
[73] Hebrews 9:4
[74] Isaiah 42:6
[75] Romans 10:2-3
[76] Romans 14:4 & 13
[77] John 14:16-21 and 16:7-11

Chapter 14: Divine Symbolism

[78] Zechariah 3:1-9 (Note: Joshua is Jesus in Greek)
[79] Leviticus 16:5-22
[80] John 13:15
[81] Ephesians 1:4-6
[82] Romans 5:6-11
[83] 2 Timothy 2:5
[84] 2 Thessalonians 2:10-12
[85] Ephesians 1:7-10
[86] Colossians 1:27 and 2:6

[87] Colossians 1:9-27
[88] Hebrews 10:26

Chapter 15: Diversity and Traditions

[89] Deuteronomy 6:4-9
[90] Romans 2:28-29
[91] Exodus 15:26
[92] Galatians 1:13-14
[93] Jeremiah 2:30
[94] Jeremiah 2:32
[95] Exodus 22:9
[96] Deuteronomy 11:26-28

Chapter 16: Children of God

[97] ref. John 8:19 & 12:44-50
[98] John 8:16-19
[99] ref. 2 Corinthians 4:4
[100] Philippians 2:6-11
[101] Galatians 3:26-29
[102] Luke 6:40
[103] 1 Timothy 2:5
[104] Matthew 10:24
[105] ref. see Mark 7:18-23
[106] Romans 8:29-30
[107] ref. John 13:15
[108] ref. Ephesians 17:21-23
[109] ref. Ephesians 3:17-21 & John 14:22-31
[110] Ephesians 2:19 & 21, 22

[111] Titus 3:6-7
[112] ref. Hebrews 8:2-6
[113] ref. Matthew 17:1-8
[114] Matthew 11:15
[115] ref. Romans 8:29
[116] ref. Isaiah 51:1
[117] ref. Job 12:7-9
[118] ref. Matthew 23:5-7
[119] Hebrews 8:2 & 4-6

Chapter 17: Let There Be Peace

[120] Genesis 13:8-9
[121] ref. Luke 7:2-10
[122] ref. Numbers 14:33
[123] ref. Isaiah 14:12-15 & Ezekiel 28:13-19
[124] ref. Matthew 23:4
[125] Matthew 15:7
[126] Matthew 23:25-28 & 23:33-36
[127] *One Tin Soldier*, Coven. Written by Dennis Lambert and Brian Potter. Billy Jack, Time Warner Entertainment Company, Burbank, CA, 1971
[128] ref. Ezekiel 7:9
[129] John 3:19-21
[130] Romans 13:12
[131] ref. Genesis 12:1-3
[132] ref. Genesis 17:1
[133] ref. Romans 4:13-25
[134] Proverbs 8:20
[135] Colossians 3:5

Notes

[136] Genesis 18:18
[137] 1 Timothy 6:18

Chapter 18: Bridging Heaven and Earth

[138] Romans 8:29
[139] Galatians 4:19-20
[140] John 13:38
[141] John 15:13
[142] Jeremiah 3:19
[143] John 13:38

Chapter 19: Clear Signs

[144] The Cow 2:94 (Al Baqarah), The Koran
[145] The Creator 35:18 (Al-Fatir), The Koran
[146] Ornaments of Gold 43:88 (Al-Zukhruf), The Koran
[147] Counsel 42:15-16 (Al-Shura), The Koran
[148] Counsel 42:13 (Al-Shura), The Koran
[149] The Greeks 30:33 (Al-Rum), The Koran
[150] The Believers 23:52 (Al-Mu'minum), The Koran
[151] The Greeks 30:41 (Al-Rum), The Koran
[152] The Table 5:66 (Al-Ma), The Koran
[153] The 'Imrans 3:144 (Al-'Imran), The Koran
[154] The Bee (Al-Nahl) 16:69, The Koran
[155] Luqman 31:27, The Koran
[156] The Bee (Al-Nahl) 16:43, The Koran

CPSIA information can be obtained
at www.ICGtesting.com
Printed in the USA
LVOW03s0402240817
546172LV00019B/401/P